GW00599078

PENGUIN BOOKS

**_Cosmopolitan_ Guide to Working in Finance**

Robert Gray is a freelance journalist who contributes to consumer magazines, national newspapers and the business press. He is co-author of the _Cosmopolitan Guide to Working in PR and Advertising_, which is forthcoming in Penguin.

# COSMOPOLITAN
## Guide to Working in
# Finance

ROBERT GRAY

PENGUIN BOOKS

PENGUIN BOOKS

Published by the Penguin Group
Penguin Books Ltd, 27 Wrights Lane, London w8 5tz, England
Penguin Books USA Inc., 375 Hudson Street, New York, New York 10014, USA
Penguin Books Australia Ltd, Ringwood, Victoria, Australia
Penguin Books Canada Ltd, 10 Alcorn Avenue, Toronto, Ontario, Canada m4v 3b2
Penguin Books (NZ) Ltd, 182–190 Wairau Road, Auckland 10, New Zealand

Penguin Books Ltd, Registered Offices: Harmondsworth, Middlesex, England

First published 1996
10 9 8 7 6 5 4 3 2 1

Set in 10.5/13pt Monotype Baskerville
Typeset by Datix International Limited, Bungay, Suffolk
Printed in England by Clays Ltd, St Ives plc

# Contents

# Chapter 1 / **Introduction**

Money, they say, makes the world go round. It is the lifeblood of any business. It is the fuel on which our economy runs and the means by which we acquire life's essentials and luxuries. Money can't buy you love ... but it *will* get you almost everything else. And because money figures large in the great scheme of things, organizations and individuals have to take their financial affairs seriously. To some degree we all depend on the services, advice and expertise offered by those who have chosen to work in a financial capacity. The question is, would you find it rewarding to be one of them?

This *Cosmo* guide will give you the answers you need to make up your mind. In the chapters that follow we will take you through the range of jobs and career paths, outlining the qualities and qualifications you need for each. And to give you a clear idea of what it's like, this book is packed with case studies of women already working in finance, who talk about their jobs in their own words. Some of these women are senior, others quite junior, but all offer an insight into the work they do and how they have gone about building their careers. There is also job-hunting advice, tips for handling interviews, pointers for getting ahead and a list of useful contact addresses. Plus there are details of relevant courses and salaries (which throughout are quoted as gross pay per year). And explanations of some of the financial jargon appear in the glossary (see p. 134).

Before we get into that, though, it is important to set the different financial careers in context, for although a career in accountancy is an alternative path to one in banking or insurance, there can be some overlap. Despite the abundant differences, there is much that links these various financial careers. Accountants often work for banks, banks advise insurance companies and insurance companies are huge investors in the City, ploughing money they manage from life-assurance premiums and pension contributions into the financial markets. In 1994 long-term investment of such funds amounted to an immense £468 billion.

The business of finance is far older and more established than many other careers you might have considered, such as advertising or information technology, and the centre of it is the City of London. Here, among the gleaming modern office blocks with their hi-tech dealing rooms, can be found a trail of tradition that winds back centuries. Did you know that the doorkeepers at the Bank of England still wear the same red and pink livery as their predecessors did when the bank was founded 300 years ago? That Lloyd's, the insurance market now located in a striking and controversial building designed by leading architect Sir Richard Rogers, was founded in a London coffee house in the seventeenth century? That the Stock Exchange was given its name in 1773? That the Corporation of London, the local authority that promotes the City, is older than Parliament? That building societies have been in existence for more than 200 years? That banking can be traced back to the Middle Ages? And that the oldest professional banking body in the world is the Chartered Institute of Bankers in Scotland, established in 1875?

Yet if you do opt for finance, you will be moving into an area which has become increasingly dynamic and which in recent years has undergone revolutionary changes. New technology and innovative approaches to the way in which financial services are delivered have transformed the industry. One of the biggest upheavals has been caused by the introduction of telephone banking, the best known example of which is First Direct, and telephone insurance services, as pioneered by Direct Line. Founded in 1985, Direct Line now employs 3,000 people and has over 2.5 million customers, most of its core business selling household and motor insurance.

The success of companies like First Direct and Direct Line has proved that consumers welcome the convenience of simply making a phone call to arrange their banking and insurance needs. It seems inevitable that many more people will favour the direct approach in the next few years. New technology is increasing the ways in which these financial services can be delivered: NatWest has been testing the viability of interactive home banking using cable television networks, and many other banks and financial companies are assessing the potential of the Internet.

New technologies and the intensity of competition in the banking and insurance sectors have led to a wave of job cuts in recent years, making it harder to get a career off the ground. Yet the changes have also brought opportunities as employers have sought new skills to complement those they have traditionally required. You need to be realistic but don't be discouraged if you hear a news report about a company laying off staff: well over a million people work in finance or finance-related jobs in the UK, and with a job pool of that size there will always be some way in which able and resolute applicants will get that all-important first job.

Women probably have a better chance now to forge an exciting and worthwhile career for themselves in finance than at any previous time. The City of London remains at present a male-dominated domain, but that is changing. Many of its banks and institutions are keen to redress the balance by recruiting women. The same holds true in insurance and personal finance, and the number of qualified female accountants has risen substantially during the last decade. While in 1985 a mere 7 per cent of the Institute of Chartered Accountants in England & Wales' 100,000-plus members were women, this had more than doubled to 15 per cent by 1994. Though it is still a pitifully low proportion, it is heartening that in every year since 1985 over 30 per cent of the ICAEW's student intake has been female. Women are obtaining professional financial qualifications in significant numbers and embarking on high-flying careers. Is there any reason why you can't do the same?

Chapter 2 looks at accountancy as a career. It takes you through the different jobs in accounting firms such as auditing, tax consultancy and insolvency practice. It also sets out the opportunities for accountants wishing to work in the public sector or in business and industry, where responsibilities can range from taking care of the payroll to calling the shots on financial strategy as the high-powered finance director of a multinational corporation.

In Chapter 3 we turn to retail banking, outlining the various roles in branch banking as well as more specialized jobs such as private and corporate banking. We tackle insurance and personal finance in Chapter 4: what is the role of an actuary? A broker? An independent financial adviser? How do you become one?

In Chapter 5 the spotlight is on the City of London, that sophisticated network of financial companies, institutions and markets that may seem bewildering and impenetrable to an outsider. We slice through the mystique and terminology to spell out what the City is all about: corporate finance, merchant banking, equity analysis, fund management, derivatives trading . . . we take you through what is involved in each career and give you the advice you need to get in and get ahead.

This guide will give you a proper understanding of what the various financial careers entail. Whichever route you decide to take, you'll need to be focused and committed to land the job you want. But, as our case histories of women working in finance prove, it can be done. We hope they will inspire you to follow in their footsteps. All that remains is to wish you career satisfaction and success. Good luck.

# Chapter 2 / **Accountancy**

Accountants make an impact on every business, institution, charity and public-sector organization in the land. Their input is essential to the smooth running of the businesses of all legitimate employers. Accountants are trained to understand the fundamentals of cash-flow and profitability that are vital to the financial well-being of an organization. Because they understand these business fundamentals so thoroughly, many accountants eventually become chief executives or senior company directors – so don't be fooled by that tired stereotype of accountants as dull wretches spending all day, every day, on book-keeping.

That is not to say that you don't need a head for figures. You certainly do – and you should enjoy solving numerical problems. You also need the gumption to study while holding down a full-time job. The training will be a test of your perseverance and stamina: it is arduous, but once you have qualified your skills will be in demand and the chances are that you won't want for a well-paid job.

Accountants are active in a wide variety of areas including the preparation of accounts, auditing, taxation, insolvency, management consultancy and corporate finance. To succeed in the profession you should be self-motivated, an adept communicator, efficient at managing your time and – more and more frequently – good at working in a team.

An accountant may work in either public practice or in business, industry and the public sector. Many gain experience on both sides of the fence.

## Public Practice

A job in public practice means working as either a self-employed accountant or for an accountancy firm. In the case of the latter these range in size from small local firms to medium-sized regional and national firms to the so-called 'Big Six', Coopers & Lybrand, KPMG Peat Marwick, Ernst & Young, Arthur Andersen, Price Waterhouse and Touche Ross. Although they face some challenges from the medium-sized firms, the Big Six dominate when it comes to large audits and insolvencies. According to the weekly trade magazine *Accountancy Age*, in 1993 these leading firms had a combined income of £2.5 billion, 170 UK offices and 32,400 professional staff.

The Big Six usually recruit undergraduates towards the end of their penultimate year or at the start of their final year at university, although they will take graduates with a year or two's work experience in another field if they feel they have something to offer. The subject of your degree is immaterial (unless it is in accountancy you will have to take a conversion course) but your academic performance matters. Trainee positions at Big Six firms are much sought-after, so the firms can afford to be choosy. Ernst & Young, for instance, specifies that applicants should have at least 22 A level points, but it prefers a minimum of 24 and its average for new recruits is 26. Between them the Big Six recruit about 2,000 graduate trainees a year.

The Big Six take part in the milk-round (initial recruitment visits that companies make to universities) but their budgets don't always stretch far enough to allow them to target any but the top universities. If you're not at one, don't let that put you off. It shouldn't leave you at a disadvantage; it simply means contacting the Big Six directly for an application form.

The attributes they look for are the will to win, get-up-and-go, confidence, the capacity to solve problems and evidence that you can work well in a team. Part of the recruitment process may involve aptitude tests, which examine numerical, cerebral and diagrammatic reasoning.

The rule of thumb in public practice is that the larger the firm the more specialist your job is likely to be. Before joining a Big Six firm you will probably be asked whether you want to specialize in audit or tax, the two main areas where training contracts are offered. Don't worry, you can change direction later on if you so wish. Starting salaries at Big Six firms are £16–17,000 in London and slightly lower elsewhere. Interest-free loans may be available to help you pay off any student debts. Starting salaries at medium-sized or small firms may be as low as £9,000.

We will look at the different specialist career paths in the Big Six and medium-sized firms later in this chapter, but first let's consider those accountants who operate as all-rounders.

## General Practice

Accountants in general practice usually work either for small accountancy firms or are self-employed. Their client base tends to be a mixture of small businesses and individuals. Just as medical general practitioners deal with all sorts of cases, an accountant in general practice works on many kinds of business. When dealing with a small company this can span the spectrum from preparing accounts to auditing, resolving questions of taxation, controlling costs or offering general commercial advice on matters such as EC law or choosing a computer system. An accountant in general practice often becomes a surrogate finance director to their clients.

The work accountants do for individuals is mainly in the area of personal/family finance, which entails giving advice on anything from inheritance or capital gains tax to insurance and pension planning, investments, wills and mortgages. Accountants in general practice will frequently be in competition for business not just with rival accountants but with other financial advisers and local solicitors too.

General practice lacks the glamour of working for the larger firms with their national and international networks, but some people find it tremendously satisfying. There is great variety to the work, you develop skills as an all-rounder and from a relatively early stage you have some say in the way the firm is run. If you have a lot to offer you may quickly be promoted to partner level. Alternatively, once you are fully qualified and have sufficient experience you may wish to set up in business on your own.

The Institute of Chartered Accountants in England & Wales (ICAEW) has a General Practitioner Board which is set up to protect and advance the interests of its members in general practice. Salaries are lower than at the bigger firms and trainees start on £10–12,000.

---

## Angeli Arora

*Age* : **23**
*Job title* : **Trainee chartered accountant**
*Employer* : **Alliotts**
*Salary* : **£12,000**
*Academic qualifications* : **BSc in accountancy (2:1), and A levels in maths, history and French**

'When I began my A levels I wasn't sure what I wanted to do so I chose three broad subjects. But my favourite subject was maths. I discussed what I should do at university with my family and we decided that it would be wise to do a professional degree because you'd be more focused after you've done it. So I did accountancy at Dundee, which was very occupationally oriented. After graduating I worked for six months as a temp in the accounts department of an advertising company. While I was there I applied for jobs at companies where I could train to become a chartered accountant. I applied to small, medium and large firms. But I got the impression that you're more of a statistic at the larger companies, so I chose a smaller company because I thought I'd prefer working there.

'In a smaller company you do a bit of everything. I've worked on accounts preparation, auditing, company-secretarial work plus the admin stuff such as photocopying and filing. You get a broad outlook that's advantageous to put on your CV. And you get to know your clients, who can be sole traders, small partnerships and even the odd big firm. In the six months I've been at Alliotts I'd say I've spent three of them outside the office at audits, client meetings and training courses. So you're not stuck in the same office all the time.

'Doing a nine-to-five job then going home and opening the books to study takes some adjusting to. It gets tough. But it's a means to an end – a qualification that's a passport to business. I think eventually I'd like to go into lecturing about accountancy. But I want to get fully qualified and get more commercial experience first.'

## Audit

It is a legal requirement for companies in the UK to have their accounts audited to demonstrate that they provide a 'true and fair' view of their financial position. Only chartered and certified accountants (that is, those belonging to the ICAEW, its sister bodies or the Association of Certified Accountants, (ACCA), see p. 104, Qualifications) are permitted to carry out audits.

Many trainees at the larger firms begin in the audit department because auditing offers a clear insight into how businesses work. As an auditor you spend much of your time with clients, learning what makes them more or less profitable, helping them to improve their systems and solve their problems.

At first auditing can be repetitive. A trainee will scrutinize a company's sales, purchases and payroll to make sure everything has been processed correctly. As your experience grows, however, the work becomes more varied and demanding, and you are given greater responsibility. That could mean doing most of the audit of a small company, or working with a team of seniors, a manager and a partner on the audit of a multinational company.

If you stay in audit at one of the large firms you will become a senior, when you will be given assignments to run and be responsible for audits, from planning through to the production of accounts. You will work closely with your clients, advise and help train junior members of staff and give regular progress reports to your managers and partners. You will have to work efficiently because the client is being billed for your time.

Starting salaries in audit range from about £17,000 at the London offices of the Big Six firms down to £12–15,000 at smaller firms and outside London. Seniors will earn a salary in the late £20,000s to early £30,000s. Junior managers at Big Six firms are paid £35–40,000 plus car.

## Taxation

Every business transaction has tax implications, and few important business decisions are taken without first considering the impact on taxation. Accountants who specialize in tax therefore make an important contribution to their clients' corporate decision-making.

The main thrust of the work is to minimize clients' tax liabilities. It often involves advising clients on how to achieve their business objectives – anything from a restructuring to an acquisition – in the most tax-efficient way, while ensuring that this fits in with their overall strategy.

A tax accountant also makes sure that clients pay all due tax. They will differentiate between transactions that are taxable and those that are not, and will work out which items are tax deductible, and recover any overpaid tax. Should there be a dispute over the amount of tax due, they will negotiate with the Inland Revenue and Customs and Excise. Working in tax involves a lot of research and analysis. Unlike auditing, much of the contact with clients is by telephone rather than face-to-face so it is not an option that appeals to those who like to get out and about. However, in the main it is better paid than auditing.

Once qualified, it is usual to specialize in certain kinds of tax, for example corporate, VAT, personal or international. Experienced tax accountants often work in a high-level consulting capacity.

Starting salaries are about £18,000 in the London offices of Big Six firms and from about £11,000 at medium-size firms outside London. Seniors at the big firms may earn £30–35,000, managers about £45,000.

---

## Jean Sharp

*Age :* **36**
*Job title :* **Tax partner**
*Employer :* **Ernst & Young**
*Salary :* **Over £75,000**
*Academic qualifications :* **BSc in commerce (1st), and the Irish Schools' Leaving Certificate in six subjects**

'After my degree I did the diploma in professional accountancy at University College Dublin and trained in audit for three years with KPMG in Dublin. I then decided that I wanted to specialize in tax and I got a job with Coopers & Lybrand – in Papua New Guinea! I really enjoyed it. I saw quite a bit of the country and travelled to the Far East. I also went on training courses in Australia. Papua New Guinea is rich in minerals so a lot of big companies are involved in mining. That was good for my career.

'After three and a half years I came back to Europe and got a job as a tax manager in the Edinburgh office of Ernst & Young. My specialization at first was large corporates but as Edinburgh has a lot of insurance companies I realized that I'd better learn a bit more about financial services as well.

'In July 1995 I was made a partner. I'm the first woman partner in the Edinburgh office, which I think is an achievement.

'I like the diversity of my job. I don't know from one day to the next what each will bring. For instance, today the Government announced it was changing the law on the taxation of executive share options. So I've been dealing with phone calls about that. Tomorrow I'm going to see a company about transfer pricing – that's looking at the tax implications of the prices it sets in different countries.

'You have to be prepared to work hard. But it's a fantastic career and I've had everything out of it. I've had the opportunity to travel and had a baby as well, about which the firm has been very supportive.'

## Insolvency

Insolvency, known in most firms by the more upbeat name corporate recovery, deals with businesses that are in financial difficulties. Sometimes this entails working with the management of a struggling business to turn it round, while on other occasions accountants are appointed by those who have lent money to the company (banks or other large creditors) to investigate the cause of its problems and advise on what should be done. This may mean recommending changes that enable the company to survive on its own, but if the problems are serious it could lead to a formal insolvency. In these cases the lenders will seek to realize their security, which may mean placing the business in administrative receivership and selling all or part of it as a going concern or, if the situation is particularly bad, winding up its affairs and selling off its assets. This latter course of action is called liquidation.

Insolvency practitioners sometimes have to investigate any wrong-doing by the directors or staff of insolvent companies. If anyone has committed a financial misdemeanour the insolvency practitioner will report it to the authorities. In some cases of financial irregularity, and if they think there is a chance of recouping some money for their clients, they may instruct a solicitor to pursue a debt. Accountants specializing in insolvency often work closely with solicitors. Insolvency practitioners need a good commercial mind and strong negotiating talent to squeeze the maximum value out of assets. You need to be able to placate and reassure disgruntled and often impatient creditors, and to motivate and console people who have seen their business dreams or personal finances turn to ashes.

It is an exciting career, which becomes more challenging and demanding the further up the ladder you get. As a receiver you are responsible for the running of a business, making decisions that affect both employees and creditors. By negotiating the sale of all or part of a company you may be able to safeguard jobs and help creditors recover what they are owed. Insolvency practitioners are also sometimes called upon to run companies that have been put into administration, which differs from receivership in that the 'administrative receiver' is appointed at the request of the company rather than its creditors. While companies that go into receivership are generally wound up (that is, cease trading permanently) those in administration can sometimes be rescued, resuming normal trading once they are back on a sound financial footing. For an insolvency practitioner it can be immensely satisfying to see a company emerge from administration that you and your colleagues have been controlling.

During the depths of the late-eighties recession, when businesses were collapsing right, left and centre, insolvency work flourished. Today there are fewer opportunities but, unfortunately for entrepreneurs and investors, a reasonably steady stream of companies will always be in need of the insolvency experts' skills.

Insolvency specialists are represented by the Society of Practitioners of Insolvency, which was formed in 1990. An insolvency practitioner needs to be licensed by a recognized professional body such as the ICAEW or the ACCA to act as an administrator, receiver or liquidator. Licences are awarded once you have passed the Joint Insolvency Examination Board's exams and have accumulated 600 hours of insolvency work experience. There are around 2,000 insolvency practitioners in the UK.

As it is an area of specialization, insolvency practitioners may be paid 5–10 per cent more than someone at a comparable level in audit. A trainee will earn £8–14,000, a senior £14–25,000, a supervisor £17–27,000 and a manager £22–40,000, though, of course, salaries vary depending on the size of the firm.

## Management and Business Consulting

Most of the bigger accountancy firms are involved in management or business consulting. Accountants working in this area apply their financial and commercial skills to give corporations and other clients advice on organizing and developing their business. They may assist a company's management in defining business objectives and strategy, or advise on a corporate restructuring to improve operational efficiency or make cost savings, or, indeed, propose the introduction of new business systems – particularly computer systems. They often compete for business against specialist firms of management consultants like McKinsey.

---

### Lisa Scherdel

*Age* : **29**
*Job title* : **Business consulting manager**
*Employer* : **Arthur Andersen**
*Salary* : **£40–45,000**
*Academic qualifications* : **BSc in banking and finance (1st) and four A levels, in French, maths, economics and general studies**

'I didn't want to work in London because I had a boyfriend up north so I applied to Arthur Andersen in Leeds. I joined in audit because it gives you good business training, plus you go out and see lots of clients. I did two years in audit and decided that I didn't want to be an audit manager. I wanted to work in a more general advisory capacity with businesses.

'At that time Arthur Andersen was setting up a business-consulting team in the Leeds office and I asked to join it. Now I'm the manager of a team of twelve. We are facilitators. A client comes to us with what they see as the problem. But it's often just the symptom. We have to convince them we can cure the symptom, then go in and solve the real problem. We look at their business and apply our experience of different processes.

'I like the variety and the challenge. At one time I was working with a TV company that needed a review of its operations and a steel stockholder which needed help with its organizational structure. I draw up work plans for our consulting seniors, people about three years my junior, and when we're at a client they'll often do the interviews to identify the problems and issues we need to look at. I may run a workshop where we get ten or fifteen people together from the client and help them find the right answers for themselves.

'You've got to be able to see the big picture and be a good communicator. And you have to have a genuine interest in a client's business. I do get a buzz out of helping them solve seemingly insoluble problems. My proudest achievement was working for part of British Coal that was being sold off. The work they were doing was being put out to tender and I think only the managing director appreciated the complexity of what they had to do to get the contract. We helped them work out the lowest possible cost for their tender. In the end they won nine out of the ten regions they bid for.

'You have to be ambitious to survive. We work for as long as it takes, and we do work pretty hard. There's no question of not being able to meet a deadline.'

## Business, Industry and Public Service

About a quarter of the top 500 companies in the UK have an accountant as their managing director or chairman, and over half of the ICAEW's 100,000-plus members work in business and industry. The Institute even has its Board for Chartered Accountants in

Business, set up to service the needs of members who work in the world of commerce.

There is a wide variety of possible jobs, with opportunities for both professionally qualified and unqualified staff. Let's start with the latter.

## Accounts Clerk

Large organizations have large accounts departments, in which many of the positions are filled by staff who have never studied accountancy. Of course, to begin with these positions may be lowly and the work repetitive, but if you get a job of this kind it will give you some idea of whether a career in finance is up your street. If you show promise and commitment you may find your employer investing time and money in developing your skills so that you become more of an asset.

It is possible to climb the corporate ladder from relatively humble beginnings, but you will be reliant on your immediate superior to spot and nurture your talent. Even if you shine, it may not be easy to stand out, particularly in large corporations where there may be fifty or more accounts clerks. You will certainly progress far more quickly if you join a company's graduate training scheme. That said, if you don't have the academic qualifications to land a training contract, a clerk's job offers a way in. Employers usually look for a minimum of four GCSEs.

Common junior jobs include positions like purchase ledger, sales ledger or payroll clerk. Sales ledger is a credit control job, the heart of which is chasing debtors for payment; purchase ledger is the other side of the coin and entails checking that goods ordered by the company have been received and that payment is made on time, although not any earlier than necessary. You need to be numerate, methodical and good at working in a team. Salaries are low at first but rise as you accumulate more experience and take on greater responsibility.

For an accounts clerk with a year or two's experience, salaries are £7–11,000 in most of the country, and £9–12,500 in the South East. An experienced accounts supervisor may earn from £10,000 upwards outside London to £13–18,000 in the capital. A payroll clerk may earn £7,500–£14,000 and a payroll manager £14–25,000.

## Finance Manager

This is a difficult job to define, not least because it varies in nature from company to company. Indeed, even its name is inconsistent. At some companies finance managers are called financial controllers and have a good deal of authority. At others they may have less leeway – especially if a management accountant is also working at the organization.

A finance manager often reports to the finance director. Typical elements of the job might be preparing statutory accounts, keeping records of the company's financial performance, presenting financial information to directors and giving opinions on investment/purchase decisions. They might also have a say in shaping the company's accounting systems and in recruiting financial staff.

There is no single path to becoming a finance manager. Some are qualified accountants, others work their way up through an organization from junior accounts positions. As you would expect, given the vast disparities in the nature of the job from one organization to another, remuneration varies. However, a finance manager can earn about £35,000.

## Finance Director

The buck stops at the finance director's desk. She has ultimate responsibility for financial matters within a corporation and usually works closely with senior colleagues on the board.

The role of a finance director differs within public and private companies. A finance director on the group board of a listed public limited company (plc) has to concern herself with following Stock Exchange practice and regulations. She will probably give briefings to City analysts, maintain contact with important investors and talk to journalists about the company's financial performance, taking care not to break the strict stock-market rules on disclosure of financial information. She and her staff will work out the best way to raise capital for expansion and acquisitions. To this end she may spend some time in liaison with investment banks and stockbrokers.

If you are a finance director at a subsidiary company of a major plc your role will have greater similarities with that of a finance manager. You will ensure that the financial reporting is accurate and timely, and will make strategic business decisions together with the subsidiary's other directors. You will also keep the group finance director up to date with trading figures and profit projections.

If you are a finance director at a private company you won't have to worry about the complexities of the City. However, your company still has to produce annual accounts and meet its targets for increasing turnover and profit. You will have the final say on most financial decisions.

For many people, becoming a finance director is the ultimate goal in their financial career, but it takes some doing. It is unusual for anyone to become a finance director of a sizeable corporation before their early thirties.

Finance directors at smaller or regional companies may be paid £30–40,000 a year, with some in the South East earning up to £50,000. Those at medium-sized companies or big divisions within larger organizations may get £35–80,000. Group finance directors at large quoted companies can earn over £100,000.

## Fiona Driver

*Age* : **32**
*Job title* : **Finance director**
*Employer* : **Kiss 100**
*Salary* : **£30–40,000**
*Academic qualifications* : **BSc in computer science and accounting (2:1), and three A levels, in maths, physics and chemistry**

'I am the finance director of Kiss 100, London's dance-music radio station. We're a subsidiary of the large media group Emap and I report to their radio division. I am responsible for the running of the accounts department, which covers the preparation of monthly management accounts, annual budgets and quarterly forecasts, cash management, credit and cost control. I am also responsible for the traffic department – advertising logs, not road reports!

'My job is to review and report rather than process transactions. I deal with the different departments within Kiss 100, and that can involve commercial decisions as well as creative input. Other aspects of my job include staff administration, computers and liaison with solicitors and official bodies.

'There are daily deadlines as advertisers can book airtime for the following day. My job is to check the price at which the airtime is sold and the credit risk. As a dance-music station we deal with promoters who, for example, may have a one-off event and it is therefore very important to get the cash up front. Kiss 100 actively seeks to extend the brand and I get involved in potential franchising deals. Currently we are looking at Kiss TV, but in what form is as yet undecided and is the subject of many brainstorming meetings to come.

'Accounting always meant that you could go into any form of business. You can step further away from accounting as your career develops and become more commercial, which I prefer. To summarize, my day is a busy one. I never know what the next phone call could be about and being in a hectic, creative environment makes accounting enjoyable.'

## Internal Audit

Large corporations have internal as well as external auditors. They are usually members of staff, although it is possible for accountancy firms to take on the internal role. Internal auditors must be qualified chartered or certified accountants.

The internal auditors' task is to establish that the corporation's internal control system is adequate and effective. They shape the overall audit strategy, that is, the planning for and delivery of the audit. They keep an eye on auditing costs, and they may have to advise on the best information systems for the job.

You need good management and communication skills and the ability to work well in a team. Internal audit managers are usually paid £25–45,000, depending on their experience and the size of the company in question. A head of internal audit at a large UK company could earn up to £60,000.

## Corporate Treasury

A treasurer's job is to manage the employer's liquidity (cash reserves) and financial risk. A major part of this is co-ordinating the organization's activities in the financial markets, arranging loan facilities with banks and examining the flow of funds within the organization and its financial structure. It is often a senior job, which involves working closely with the finance director.

Many large companies now have treasury departments, but corporate treasury is a small profession – the Association of Corporate Treasurers has fewer than 2,000 members – and it isn't an easy one to enter. Most treasurers begin work in a corporation's accounts/finance department and move on to become a treasury assistant where they begin their training. Most accountants don't begin to train in this area until they reach their late twenties or early thirties.

A group treasurer at a major UK company could earn anywhere between £40,000 and £80,000.

## Management Accounting

Management accountants contribute to the formulation of company strategy. They compile and interpret the financial information companies need to make informed and sensible business decisions. They compare financial predictions with what has actually happened, and monitor sales and profit trends. Their work is to check that resources are being used efficiently and that the various parts of a business are providing value for money.

Roles vary from employer to employer, but as a management accountant you may be responsible for the preparation of monthly management accounts, cash-flow predictions, annual budgets, statutory accounts, costings and a variety of management statistics. You may have to plan and review the systems that produce this information, and recommend and implement any changes. You may also have a say on issues such as product/service pricing and salaries.

A management accountant may earn anywhere between £18,000 and 40,000, depending on the size and location of the company. A senior management accountant at a large firm may earn up to £48,000.

## Carol Hewitt

*Age* : **40**
*Job title* : **Management accountant**
*Employer* : **Thames Water Utilities**
*Salary* : **£26,000**
*Academic qualifications* : **BSc in pure maths (2:2), and three A levels, in pure maths, applied maths and physics**

'I have our head office to look after, which includes support departments like research and development, environment and external relations. I'm not responsible for the operations side of the business, which is the part dealing with sewage and supplying water.

'I produce quarterly forecasts, which take a couple of weeks to put together. I see people in the various departments and go through what they're doing to produce forecasts for their operating costs, and income where they have it. I also do the monthly management accounts, which show what they're spending against budgets and forecasts. I highlight any problems that have to be addressed and present the information at a monthly meeting of directors and senior management.

'I have to make sure that every department knows what it is spending its money on. There's quite a bit of educating to be done because these aren't finance people. It's a question of helping them to get their budget sorted out. It's more than just financial advice, it's total business advice to help them improve their situation.

'You have to be able to communicate and take things slowly to make sure they understand. A lot of people don't have too much of an idea about what to do so after you've helped them it's good to see them manage and come up with decent financial information.

'There is a lot of routine in this job, so you've got to be prepared for some repetition. But I do get away from my desk quite a lot. You have to be quite meticulous and ensure that you're giving accurate information because people are relying on it. And you've got to monitor expenditure against what has been planned. I'm a certified accountant, which is a good qualification to have.'

## Public Service Accountant

The extensive privatizations of recent years have slimmed down the public sector in this country, yet it remains a major employer – for accountants as well as for planning officers, police constables and Whitehall bureaucrats. Some accountants choose to specialize in public service, working for public-sector employers such as central or local government and the National Health Service. They may also work for the privatized utilities that provide a public service such as British Gas, BT and the regional water and electricity companies.

Due to the unique demands attached to working in the public sector, many of the accountants who do so have qualified with the Chartered Institute of Public Finance and Accountancy (CIPFA, see p. 105, Qualifications), which is specifically geared to a career in public service.

Public service accountants often face stringent budget constraints: it is down to them as financial managers to make sure the public gets value for money. In other words, they have to implement solutions which are low-cost and effective. They also need to be commercially aware: many public-sector services are now 'outsourced' (that is, tendered out) to private-sector contractors so the accountant needs an understanding of public/private-sector partnerships.

Trainee salaries begin at about £8,000. Graduate trainees tend to be paid £10–16,000. Recently qualified public service accountants may earn £15–25,000, chief accountants £25–40,000, assistant treasurers/deputy directors of finance £27–46,000, treasurers/directors of finance £35–80,000.

## Getting In and Getting Ahead

The overwhelming majority of professionally qualified accountants are graduates, and the trend towards recruiting trainees with
degrees is gathering momentum. With demand for training contracts far outstripping supply, employers can afford to be choosy
about whom they take on. They are, after all, going to reward the
successful candidate with a reasonably well-paid job that leads to a
first-rate business qualification. About 90 per cent of those studying to be chartered accountants are graduates, and there is a high
percentage of graduates among those studying for the qualifications of the other approved bodies.

Most of the larger accountancy firms offer training contracts to
students in their final year at university. Some attend careers fairs;
with others you will have to take the initiative and seek them out.
Contact the ICAEW, which produces an annual list of training
vacancies. Talk to your local Careers Service office if you are
interested in joining a small firm.

Employers are looking for good A-level results and a likely 2:1
degree. Any work experience is an advantage. Accountancy is all
about business, and if you have worked you will have some insight,
no matter how small, into the business world. The personal qualities employers want are intelligence, adaptability, application and
stamina. The last two are of special importance during the three
years of the graduate training contract. Marrying the demands of
work with the need to study for tough examinations requires determination and commitment, and although most students pass
first time, it is far from easy.

One question to ask at interview is whether the employer will
pay the bulk of your training costs and give you paid study leave.
Most will, but check because they are under no obligation to do so.
You may also want to find out whether tuition for the exams is on
block release or a link programme (short bursts of tuition between
work).

Since 1 March 1995 it has been possible for good A-level students to enter directly into a four-year chartered accountancy training contract. This has come about because of worries that the profession might be losing potentially good accountants apprehensive of going to university for fear of getting into debt. Good A-level results are necessary, but a word of warning: the initiative is still in its preliminary stages and has yet to gain wide acceptance among accountancy firms. You are also eligible to enter a four-year training contract if you have a relevant BTec, HNC or HND.

There is one out-of-the-ordinary recruitment scheme that deserves mention: every year since the mid-1980s Big Six firm Arthur Andersen has been running a sponsorship programme open to outstanding sixth-form students. The scheme, which is restricted, sadly, to a mere forty places a year, gives the students nine months' paid work experience at the firm once they have finished their A levels. At the end of this period they are given a lump sum of over £1,000 with the recommendation that they use it to travel round the world. Arthur Andersen then contributes over £1,000 a year to subsidize the students' degree courses and provides them with six weeks' paid work every summer. On graduation, the students are offered jobs at the firm.

The career path within the bigger firms of accountants is clearly signposted. If you have the ability and desire to stay within public practice you can rise from assistant to senior to supervisor, manager, senior manager and, if you're talented enough, partner. Outside public practice the picture is hazier. You will have to work out where you want to be and the best way of getting there. For instance, do you want to be the finance director of a regional company or a management accountant at a division of a multinational conglomerate? Or, perhaps, the treasurer of a local authority or a finance manager at a retail group?

If you have your sights set on making it to the top of the tree in commerce or industry, you should bear in mind that the vast majority of finance directors or senior finance managers at the top companies are professionally qualified accountants, predominantly with the ICAEW (or its sister bodies), the ACCA or the Chartered Institute of Management Accountants (CIMA). All are widely respected qualifications, although in some quarters chartered accountancy is still seen as the more prestigious of the three.

If you are already working in a junior position in accounts and think you would like to make a career of it but don't have a degree or any professional qualifications, then ask your employer whether they would be prepared to sponsor you through the Association of Accounting Technicians (AAT) training scheme. It can't hurt to ask, as long as you do it pleasantly. If the answer is a vehement 'no' and they are dismissive of your abilities without good reason, you should perhaps consider finding a job with an employer more prepared to help you develop your career. If the answer is yes it could open up a panorama of possibilities.

AAT is a well-regarded qualification in its own right: experienced technicians often hold down supervisory jobs. But it can also be used as a stepping stone to becoming a professional accountant. With an AAT qualification you would be eligible for a three-year professional accountancy training contract, just as graduates are. It's no picnic, though. The AAT recommends that students should have at least two A levels, so you should have confidence in your ability to pass.

Whichever way you begin your career in accountancy, you will need to be dedicated and develop good team and communication skills to get ahead. And if you are thinking about accountancy as an option for the first time, put any thoughts of it being uniform and dreary out of our head. How many other careers allow you to work for almost any kind of company or organization?

# Chapter 3 / **Banking**

Not so long ago the high street banks and building societies could be relied on to recruit school leavers in their thousands every year. A banking job, once you got one, virtually set up you in a safe career for life. That, most definitely, no longer applies.

Today, although retail banking still offers a fine career path, the opportunities are fewer. There are a number of reasons why. New technology such as desktop computers and ATMs (cash-dispensing machines) has made branches more efficient and enabled them to cut back on staff. Telephone banking has also hit the branch structure, with many consumers preferring the convenience of talking to their banks without having to pop down to the high street. Probably most damaging of all, though, has been the intensity of the competition between rival banks and building societies as they have striven to grow and attract capital. As they have jockeyed for position a spate of takeovers and mergers has been executed with a view to increasing efficiency and profitability, one result of which has been a wave of branch closures. Since 1990, according to the Banking, Insurance and Finance Union, over 2,000 branches have closed and more than 100,000 jobs have been lost – a staggering number. Add to this the effects of the late-eighties recession and that many banks have increased their use of part-time staff, and you could be forgiven for harbouring a gloomy outlook on the prospects for a career in banking.

You would be right not to expect to waltz into a job, but don't dismiss banking without further thought. Although the banks aren't hiring nearly as many staff as they did in the past, they are still searching for talented young blood. In a tight marketplace, they need to look to the future. And the future should see a continuation in what can fairly be called a banking revolution.

The trend towards telephone banking seems set to continue, but trials are already under way into the feasibility of banking on the Internet and using cable TV networks to provide banking on demand. Then there is the prospect of 'smart cards' which one day, some pundits think, may replace cash. In the future such cards will be charged up with electronic money units at ATMs or over the telephone. The units could then be spent in shops. In the summer of 1995 the first smart card, Mondex, was introduced experimentally to consumers in Swindon.

Paradoxically, although this new technology may lead to a further reduction in the number of branches, the human touch is of greater value than ever. Customers coming into a branch expect to receive a first-rate service, which puts interpersonal skills at a premium. Selling skills are also valued and in demand. Banks and building societies need to sell financial products, ranging from basic travel insurance to mortgages, to make the investment in running an expensive branch network financially viable.

The bigger banks are also active in areas such as corporate finance and dealing on the capital markets, but these operations are distinct from their retail activities and are covered at length in Chapter 5 on the City. It is important to understand that there is much more to banking than sitting behind a counter in a branch. And it is worth remembering that bank employees generally get valuable perks like preferential loan and mortgage rates.

One last point before we look at the various jobs in retail banking: every now and again a building society talks about converting itself into a bank. What is the difference between the two? Banks are companies owned by their shareholders while building societies are 'friendly' societies run by trustees and mutually owned by their depositors. They use the money deposited by small savers, their account holders, to lend to homebuyers. At present, over 7 million people are buying homes of their own using building-society mortgages. The friendly society concept was born over two hundred years ago when a group of working people suffering bad housing conditions clubbed together to build houses for themselves. Today's large societies, like the Halifax, have grown from those roots.

## High Street Branch Jobs

Clerk/Trainee

This is the most junior grade in branch banking. It is poorly paid and offers a low level of responsibility, but at the same time it provides a good grounding in banking procedures and, for those with potential, the chance to gain experience and move up.

Typically, the job involves dealing with the daily correspondence of the branch and assorted clerical duties. Examples of this kind of work are sorting cheques and mail, filing and maintaining records, photocopying and faxing documents, and data inputting. Typing skills are a real advantage. You may also have to answer phone calls from customers and senior staff located outside the branch. These days, bank clerks are often known as bank officers.

Cashier/Customer Service Officer

The cashier or customer service officer is the first point of contact between the customer and the high street bank or building society. As such, the job is essential to the delivery of a good service.

He or she works as a receptionist or behind the counter, dealing with customer requests, handling account and investment enquiries, helping customers to pay in cheques, transfer money or set up standing orders. They maintain the ATMs and issue debit cards, and will also be trained to draw the attention of customers to new financial products or services that may be of interest to them and to try to sell services like travellers' cheques.

The job also entails checking standing orders and other transactions, some data inputting and balancing the till at the end of the working day. Experienced cashiers are often given a supervisory role, which involves organizing other branch staff. They will also be given responsibility for more complex branch banking tasks, like handling requests for small loans or overdrafts and buying and selling foriegn currency.

Cashiers must be numerate, able to communicate clearly, and have the tact and sensibility to handle difficult customers – although, of course, training will be given on how to do this.

---

## Helen Johnson

*Age* : **33**
*Job title* : **Senior customer services officer**
*Employer* : **TSB**
*Salary* : **£15,000**
*Academic qualifications* : **Three A levels, in English, French and Spanish**

'At school I was not certain which career I wanted to pursue. After my A levels, although I didn't actively plan a move into banking, I applied for a job with the TSB and was successful in securing a position. At the moment I work at the Yardley, Birmingham, branch. I get in at about eight forty-five and from then until about nine thirty is the key time. There are twenty-two staff and it's down to me to make sure they're organized to provide an efficient service. That means arranging a work plan so that everyone knows what they'll be doing that day and also when they can go to lunch.

'I have to forecast how much cash everyone needs. I also have to make sure the Speedbank machines [ATMs] have been loaded with cash and have enough stationery in them. I make sure the branch is tidy, review security and check that there are enough leaflets out. I don't do all this myself, I co-ordinate it.

'At nine thirty I have a meeting with the branch manager, service manager and assistant manager where we discuss personnel issues and look at any bank directives or new procedures that need to be implemented. The four of us are classed as the lending officers as we have the authority to make the various decisions during the day to approve or decline lending propositions.

'From about ten o'clock onwards I turn my attention to administrative duties, such as interviewing customers, answering queries or dealing with overdraft applications. It is vital that I identify any financial need a customer may have, and if I am unable to meet the requirements myself, refer the customer to one of our advisers who can help.

'There's a lot of variety in my job and the hours are good. If you're career-minded there are plenty of steps up the ladder. Personally I'm quite comfortable with the level I've reached.'

## Personal Financial Adviser

This is a highly trained job, which involves giving specialist financial advice to consumers. Personal financial advisers explain and sell quite complicated financial instruments such as mortgages, investment products and insurance policies. It is a highly competitive area because, in some respects, the banks are competing for business among themselves *and* with other financial institutions. Consequently, staff working in this area must be intelligent and able. You will have to acquire a detailed grasp of different financial products and be able to explain them concisely and honestly to members of the public. At the same time you will have performance targets to meet and will be expected to bring in business.

However, the financial services sector is becoming ever more stringently patrolled and regulated to safeguard consumers from being given erroneous advice or being sold inappropriate products, and the banks have to comply with the guidelines of regulatory bodies. This means ensuring that anyone who offers financial advice is properly qualified to do so, with one of the statutory qualifications: the Financial Planning Certificate, the Certificate for Financial Advisers (CeFA) or the Investment Advice Certificate (see p. 107, Qualifications).

The job is known by a number of different names, including financial-services adviser or even mortgage adviser.

## Branch Manager

The branch manager runs the high street retail unit. Depending on its location, this might employ a handful of staff or, in a few cases, up to 200 or more. As the branch is the bank's interface with its customers, it is essential that it offers a good service. The manager is directly responsible for providing this, for managing and caring for staff, the security of the branch and the management-trainee schemes taking place there. They are accountable for branch performance and will report to a regional manager or director. The role encompasses business development and they will approve large loans and monitor unusual transactions. In addition, they will still see customers to offer advice and encourage them to bring additional business to the branch in terms of investing their savings or taking out loans. They will also visit customers outside the branch, perhaps to view property proposed as security for a loan or to form a judgement on a small business that has requested a capital injection from the bank.

As a manager you need to motivate staff so that they are happy in their work and ensure that they can meet their targets, especially the personal financial advisers. With increased competition making banks and building societies more customer-focused, today's bank manager is a far cry from the crusty, unapproachable figure much parodied in the past. More than ever, people skills are required.

## Deborah Holmes

*Age* : **28**
*Job title* : **Branch manager**
*Employer* : **Abbey National Building Society**
*Salary* : **£25,000**
*Academic qualifications* : **BA (Hons) in business studies (2:1), and two A levels, in general studies and history**

'I travelled round the world for a year, visiting Thailand, Hong Kong, Australia, New Zealand and the States, and even worked at the Sydney National Opera House for a couple of months. In January 1991 I started on Abbey National's graduate management-trainee scheme in the Christchurch, Dorset, branch.

'During the first eighteen months I did everything from opening the post and making the coffee to serving customers and seeing if there were any savings or investment products they might be interested in. The first part of the training was very much about getting to know the Abbey National culture. Then I moved to Poole where I trained as a personal financial adviser, advising on pensions, mortgages and investments. After that I was acting branch manager in Dorchester and then applied for a secondment role as acting manager for Summertown, Oxford. I was there for a year and was then appointed a permanent branch manager. To become a permanent branch manager you have to go through a selection programme, which includes role-playing to teach you how to deal with staff and to handle difficult situations.

'As part of my career development, I decided I'd like to try something else, so I've just finished a stint as a senior management development adviser, looking at designing development programmes for managers. That included getting involved in some career counselling and gave me exposure to our head office in Milton Keynes.

'At the moment I'm the manager of the Reading, King's Road, branch. I report to an area sales manager who is also female – so there is hope! Our sales advisers have targets to meet. I still sell and have a personal target but I'm also responsible for the whole figure, and at the end of the day the priority is the branch target. Two other sales people report to me, plus a customer-service manager and about twelve other staff.

'It can be quite stressful but it's very exciting. Every day is different. You have to be flexible, determined and focused. And communications skills are quite important. I feel I've done pretty well in a short time and I wouldn't rule out a move to head office eventually.'

## Regional and Head Office Jobs

Branch managers generally report to a branch controller or regional manager who has responsibility for a number of branches, perhaps ten or fifteen. The controller/regional manager's job is to monitor the performance of each branch, suggest ways in which this could be improved to the branch managers, and ensure that all of the bank's products and services are being properly offered to its customers.

Controllers/regional managers report to an area director, who will assess the performance of the branches and the regions under their control and act as the vital connection between head office and the branches.

Many of those working at regional or head office will have begun their careers in the branch network, but there are opportunities in marketing, IT, personnel and secretarial functions for those who have no direct experience of retail banking.

The banks also employ office staff in their card services divisions, who deal with customers' credit card bills. Jobs here range from junior clerical work to taking telephone enquiries, amending a customer's borrowing limit, cancelling and replacing lost cards, tackling fraud and debt collection. The work may involve delicately reminding a customer who has forgotten to pay their bill or trying to track down someone who has disappeared without paying their outstanding debts.

## Julie Eyden

*Age* : **28**
*Job title* : **Assistant product manager**
*Employer* : **Barclays Bank**
*Salary* : **£17,000**
*Academic qualifications* : **Eight O levels (GCSEs)**

'I've always worked for Barclays. I started off in the "machine room" when I was sixteen, processing cheques and account credits and debits. I became an assistant supervisor and I've done some cashiering and been a personal banker as well, handling general enquiries from customers face-to-face and helping them open accounts. Then I went on to be a student business officer, dealing with higher education students and graduates, and had a portfolio of accounts to look after for students at Coventry University. I'd give them any help I could, liaising with the student union and university staff. I felt I was getting really close to the students, developing an empathy with them and becoming their friend. It was brilliant.

'After that I was a loans officer and a sales manager's assistant, coaching staff on providing a better customer service. Now I'm in my first management position, working in the head office marketing department. I develop products for students and graduates and deal with some of the advertising and marketing. As part of my role I go out to our regional offices and do presentations to our student business officers. Because I've done the job myself I'm comfortable presenting to the student business officers and I love going out with videos and slides.

'Barclays carries out a student debt survey every year and I help to brief the market research agency to do that. We also do a lot of research to find out what students need from a bank. I report to the youth market manager and go on marketing training courses. There are certainly a lot of prospects for me now, either in the youth team or other areas. This job is excellent. It's exciting being at the sharp end where what you do influences the products offered nationally.'

## Telephone Banking Representatives

Telephone banking has been a factor in the reduction of branch vacancies but it has created opportunities of its own for those wishing to work in what is also called direct banking.

Most of the transactions, such as balance enquiries and setting up standing orders, are handled by 'frontline' telephone representatives, who take calls from customers who identify themselves with passwords. More complex enquiries, such as requests for financial advice on loans or mortgages, are transferred to specialists.

Clearly, a frontline representative needs a good telephone manner and to be an effective communicator. You must be able to stay calm and unruffled when dealing with callers and be prepared to build up a good knowledge of the bank's products and services. Before you are allowed to deal with customers on the phone you will be given training on banking procedures and telephone techniques.

---

### Angela Eakhurst

*Age* : **25**
*Job title* : **Team coach**
*Employer* : **First Direct**
*Salary* : **£13,200**
*Academic qualifications* : **Three A levels, in French, Spanish and home economics**

'I began my career working for a high street bank, doing back-office work like opening accounts, setting up standing orders and dealing with returned cheques. I moved to a supervisor's job in processing at a large branch in Leeds, but I wasn't sure what I wanted to do. After a while I felt my career was getting stuck in a rut.

'Then I saw an ad for First Direct, the bank that offers the services of a high street bank over the phone. I joined in January 1994 as a banking representative. First of all I went on a seven-week training course, learning how to take customer calls and deal with things like paying bills, arranging standing orders and transfers over the phone. It taught me a lot about communication skills, was fun and prepared me for the banking-representative job.

'In December 1994 I took the new position of team coach. About half of my time is spent as before, taking customer calls as a banking representative. The other half I spend giving additional training to other representatives. I teach them what to do when, for example, customers want to increase their overdrafts or Visa limits, open additional cheque accounts or order travellers' cheques – the kind of things that can't be learnt within the initial seven-week training course. I also coach them on advising customers – for instance, suggesting that a customer who keeps a lot of money in a cheque account may be better off opening a savings account as well, and making sure customers are kept informed about new products and services.

'There are about a dozen people in a team here. I'm responsible for making sure everyone in my team gets refresher training whenever they need it. I like the feeling you get from training someone so that, after a few hours, they know all they need to know about a subject and are confident in handling customer queries about it.

'You need to be sociable, open and honest. Feedback is encouraged and if you've got an opinion you voice it. I'm glad I came here and feel I'm moving in the right direction. I'm just kicking myself for not having come here sooner!'

## Corporate and International Bankers

The retail banks' corporate-banking divisions work with businesses that are too large and demanding to be served effectively by high street banking staff and too small to need the regular services of the City investment banks. Such companies have an annual turnover of anywhere between £1 million and £130 million.

Corporate bankers usually work in teams serving a particular geographical area, which can be small or quite large depending on the concentration of clients. It is their job to find out about the business needs of their corporate customers and identify how the bank can best serve them. NatWest, for example, has 130 corporate banking centres across the country staffed by 350 corporate managers. Each manager has forty or fifty clients to look after. It is as much a part of their job to offer business advice as to provide banking services.

To be an effective corporate banker you must be interested in how businesses function and the people who run them. You need good interpersonal skills, and a knowledge of financial services and how they can be tailored to fit a client's needs. You also need to be a good negotiator. Some banks like their corporate-relationship staff to study for the advanced qualification of the Association of Corporate Treasurers (ACT, see p. 106, Qualifications, Accountancy) to give them a detailed knowledge of corporate cash-flow and financial management.

Banks also have international divisions to serve the cross-border requirements of their clients. Most international division staff are based in the UK but there are some opportunities to work abroad. The activities of a bank's international division include transferring international payments, financing imports and exports and advising on overseas markets. It hardly needs saying that languages are helpful if you are seeking an international division job.

## Private Banking Executives

The leading banks' private banking operations are small in comparison with their ordinary branch networks but they have been growing in size and significance in recent years. Private banking operations look after what are known as 'high net worth' individuals – or, to put it more bluntly, the well-off. This usually means people with liquid assets of £100,000 or more. A good, if frivolous, analogy is that for consumers to belong to a private bank is like staying in a luxury hotel rather than a B-and-B: they are pampered and well looked-after but pay more for the privilege. The bank makes a management charge of, say, 1 per cent of the value of a customer's portfolio. The crux of private banking is about developing relationships, making customers feel that they and their investments are in safe hands.

Private banking operations employ executives or relationship managers to look after their customers' needs. This involves updating them on the status of their accounts and investments, finding out about their financial objectives and giving advice on how to achieve them, talking them through investment opportunities and offering the latest information on new products and services. Some customers give their private banks free rein to make investment decisions for them and these decisions have to be justified if they go wrong or under-perform the average for the investment market. Equally, if the bank fails to invest their money in something that proves to be a roaring success, customers will also want to know why.

Relationship managers will look after a comparatively small number of clients. Because their clients are investing large sums through the bank they are highly valued, and relationship managers will travel to see them if that suits the customers better than coming into the office. Relationship managers need to be able to inspire confidence and trust among their customers and h keep up to date on the latest financial products and activity investment markets. They don't carry out the investment transactions themselves: this is usually done by an investment specialist or unit at the bank. Private banking operations also employ staff to generate new business.

---

## Liz McCarthy

*Age* : **24**
*Job title* : **Private banking executive**
*Employer* : **Lloyds Private Banking**
*Salary* : **£21,000**
*Academic qualifications* : **BSc in geography (2:1) and four A levels, in biology, chemistry, geography and general studies**

'Lloyds Private Banking Ltd looks after high-net-worth individuals, people with liquid assets of over £75,000. We look after their banking needs and give them independent financial advice. We're owned by Lloyds Bank plc but operate completely separately.

'I work in the Croydon office, which serves the area from the south of London out as far as Gravesend. I have 160 clients to look after, most of whom tend to be people over forty who've either inherited money or accumulated it during their working lives. I sit down with them to decide their priorities and objectives.

'Most clients have equity portfolios, but our work extends to looking at other investment options like Tessas or gilts. We also advise on tax planning, making a will and other areas of financial planning. It's my job to know the specifics, such as whether a client doesn't want to invest in certain types of shares like tobacco or alcohol companies. I'm one of three private banking executives in the office. The service is highly personal, tailored to individual clients' needs. I meet every one of my clients at least once a year for an annual financial review, but when they want to see me is entirely up to them. We're there to be used as much or as little as they want.

'After university I applied for jobs on the retail side at the four big banks. Lloyds Bank interviewed me and then came back to say they thought I was more suitable for a job in private banking and would I like one? I started off working in Birmingham, then Leeds, and had a spell at Head Office in Haywards Heath. As for professional qualifications, I've got the Securities Institute's Investment Advice Certificate.

'I report to the office manager and have a team of two working with me who handle enquiries when I'm out seeing clients and take care of the admin side of things.

'It's very rewarding building up relationships. Some clients will ring to tell you their news, such as when they've had a new grandchild. I really do enjoy working with clients. I'd like to broaden my management skills to be able to run an office while maintaining client contacts.'

## Factoring

Barclays, Lloyds, Midland, NatWest and Royal Bank of Scotland all operate in this area, as do a number of other banks and companies. Factors make money by helping companies with their cash-flow. They offer two main services: factoring and invoice discounting, both of which involve providing finance secured against a company's outstanding invoices.

Essentially, the factors buy a client's invoices as they are issued. They immediately pay the client about 80 per cent of the value of the invoice, then pay the balance once the invoice has been settled. Simply advancing the money is known as invoice discounting. In many cases the factors will also assume responsibility for the administration of the client's sales ledger and credit management, which broader service is itself known as factoring. Factors make a loan charge on the money they advance, much like a bank overdraft, and may take a fee of between 1 and 3 per cent of the value of each invoice to cover their factoring work.

There are jobs in factoring for sales staff, account managers and junior administrative staff. It is the job of the sales staff to sell the concept of factoring to businesses. Often they are not competing against other factors but against alternative means of finance, such as bank overdrafts. It is down to them to convince company directors and accountants of the benefits offered by factoring. Most sales staff tend to be graduates, and many factors prefer to recruit sales staff who are aged between twenty-five and thirty-five and already have some selling experience, which, with the ability to relate to clients, is invariably more important than having a degree.

Account managers, who may also be called client or relationship managers, look after the interests of existing clients. It is up to them to make sure that the client is happy with the service it is receiving. Some account managers join as graduate trainees but others move up from junior positions. Factors need staff to carry out administrative work and to issue gentle reminders to companies about paying invoices. Jobs such as this go to well-qualified school-leavers – the more good GCSEs or A levels you have the better – and, for the industrious and capable, offer a pathway to more senior positions.

Factoring is not a major area of employment – the top factors employ hundreds rather than thousands of staff – but because the business is growing there are opportunities. The total value of invoices handled by factors during the first six months of 1995 was 28 per cent up on the first half of 1994.

## Getting In and Getting Ahead

Most people begin their retail-banking careers in a branch, although for some graduates, administration and support staff this need not be the case. Broadly speaking, there are four different entry points: graduate, accelerated, standard and secretarial.

The banks have pruned back their graduate recruitment but not as severely as at other entry points, recognizing that they need to maintain a steady drip-feed of talent to ensure they have good managers in the future. Graduates are taken on to be groomed as future managers, and the banks look for evidence of leadership and teamwork qualities when recruiting. They also expect a good honours degree, usually a 2:2 or better. It may be in any subject although candidates with business or finance will have a slight advantage. Your personal characteristics and what you have to offer are also important. The kind of attributes that are highly sought-after are motivational traits, empathy and understanding, flexibility, analytical skills, numeracy, commercial awareness, computer literacy, the ability to communicate and the strength of character to make tough decisions.

There may be as many as a hundred applicants for each graduate-training scheme position, so you will have to prove your worth. But don't be discouraged. These jobs have to be filled, so why shouldn't one of them go to you?

The selection process normally begins on the university milk-round with an initial interview and perhaps some psychometric testing. If a bank you wish to join doesn't come to your campus, write to their graduate recruitment manager requesting an application form. If you are successful at the initial interview the next step is to be invited to the bank's assessment centre. Here, you will take part in a number of activities, ranging from group discussions and team-building exercises to analysis of case studies and devising solutions to business problems.

Some of the banks have a two-tier graduate recruitment system wherein the best candidates join a fast-track scheme, grooming them for a rapid rise to management and, if they're good enough, ultimately to director level. You should find out whether the bank to which you are applying operates a fast-track scheme – probably called something like the Advanced Development Programme – alongside its standard graduate-training scheme.

Graduate training programmes typically last between eighteen months and three years. Trainees will usually be rotated through a number of different branch jobs to get an overview of how the banking system works. There will also be regular banking and management courses. Day release study for Chartered Institute of

Bankers (CIB) qualifications will play an important part in the training. Graduate starting salaries are £12,500–16,000. A first junior management appointment may pay £17–18,000. Branch managers, depending on their experience and the size of their branch, will be paid £20–40,000. It is possible for graduates to become managers within five years.

Accelerated entry is mainly for candidates with at least two A-level passes. A BTec National Diploma in Business and Finance or GNVQ Advanced will also be considered, and some banks even take on graduates at this level. Accelerated programmes are designed to offer a fast track to senior clerical status and as such they are management-development schemes. While they offer an excellent grounding in banking and the chance of promotion through the banking grades, those taking part will not rise as quickly as graduates. Accelerated trainees will initially be paid between £6,500 and £8,000.

Standard entry is in the junior clerical positions. Experience counts here, and if you want to get in it is a good idea to find some part-time or temporary work experience. A foot in the door can often lead to a full-time job. Banks are flexible on academic qualifications at the standard-entry level but usually prefer to take those with GCSEs grade A–C in maths and English. They also look for people with computer skills, a good telephone manner and the ability to deal satisfactorily with customers. Starting salaries are £5,700 to £7,000.

The vacancies at secretarial level are mostly as secretaries to senior managers.

The qualifications of the Chartered Institute of Bankers are growing in importance, and the more of these you obtain, the better your chances of furthering your career. This requires some self-sacrifice on your part as you will have quite a lot of studying to do out of office hours.

If you are looking to get ahead quite quickly you should also be prepared to relocate to different towns and even different regions of the country, particularly in the early stages of your career. You may damage your long-term career aspirations if you turn down a promotion opportunity that means moving from where you live.

Finally, keep up to date with what the banks are doing by reading the business pages of the national newspapers. If a retail bank is launching a telephone-banking arm it will probably mean job opportunities. Follow this up. Apply direct – the retail banks rarely use employment agencies to fill junior positions. And keep a look-out for job advertisements in the quality national newspapers.

It is an exciting time for banking. And if it seems a career ready-made for you, don't let the job losses of recent years sap your confidence and determination. Go for it!

# Chapter 4 / **Insurance and Personal Finance**

In the UK, over 300,000 people work in insurance and personal finance for a range of different employers – insurance companies, insurance brokers, Lloyd's of London, reinsurance companies and loss adjusters – or, indeed, on their own as independent financial advisers.

It is reasonable to say that insurance has something of an image problem. It is still perceived as somewhat dull, staid and almost Dickensian in comparison with other careers such as IT, the media, advertising or investment banking. This may be true, to an extent: some of the junior jobs can be repetitive, although now that desktop computers hold sway the picture of put-upon clerks searching endlessly through stacks of dusty folders can be largely consigned to history. The information age has made the foothills of insurance a far more pleasant place from which to begin a career ascent.

One of the great equalizers of a career in insurance is that you don't need to be a graduate to get to the top. With one or two exceptions (actuaries are mainly graduates), jobs are open to school-leavers. Many insurance companies do not set minimum academic standards when recruiting, although most look for GCSEs in English and maths. As the industry strives to become more efficient a trend is developing towards hiring better-qualified staff, and indeed, most of the leading insurance companies offer graduate recruitment programmes for fast-track managerial career development. Although you can work your way up without a degree, graduates are likely to progress more quickly than non-graduates.

Another point to bear in mind is that professional qualifications are now far more widespread and valued than ever before. Industry bodies, employers and regulators are placing growing emphasis on passing professional examinations as evidence of competence. If you are serious about moving up the career ladder in insurance, you should reconcile yourself to studying for some professional qualifications.

## Insurance Companies

Insurance companies offer two main kinds of insurance: life and general. Life assurance is taken out by people as cover for sudden death so that their families or other beneficiaries do not suffer financially should the worst come to the worst. Life policies can be used to build up a nest egg for retirement; pensions also come into this category. Due to the complexities of and special issues relating to life assurance, it is usually separated from general business.

General insurance subdivides neatly into two: personal and commercial. Personal accounts for about half of all insurance in the UK. It is mainly motor and household insurance, providing cover for car accidents, burglary, and property damage. Commercial insurance offers cover for everything from damage to business premises and injury to employees in the workplace to protection against liability if a company has caused loss or suffering through negligence. The professional indemnity insurance taken out by doctors, lawyers and other professionals is an example of the latter.

Insurance companies are huge investors in shares, bonds and property and employ people to manage these investments (see Chapter 5 on the City). In this section we will look at jobs unique to or predominating in insurance.

Actuary

An actuary uses mathematical concepts to solve technical problems, and ensures that an insurance company charges sound premiums, pays value for money and stays solvent. The job involves applying statistics, theories of probability and interest calculations to financial affairs – mainly life assurance, mortgages and pension schemes. Within the big life-assurance companies, actuaries calculate premiums and interest rates.

Actuarial work is computer-based. You analyse figures, tackle numerical problems and set out your findings in a report. You need to be good at sharing information as well as having first-rate mathematical and management skills. There is also scope for creativity: you may be involved in developing and pricing new products, part of which may entail running profit tests to ascertain whether a product is commercially viable, or, at a more senior level, helping to formulate company policy and investment strategy. In a nutshell, you make decisions about what is likely to happen in the future. Quite a skill.

About 60 per cent of actuaries work for insurance companies, on both life and other business – and, indeed, every insurance company must have what is known as an appointed actuary, whose role is to make sure the company has sufficient assets to meet future commitments. To do this, the actuary undertakes regular valuations of the company to make sure it is not going to go bust, and recommends how much money is available to pay policyholders in bonuses, dividends to shareholders, and how much to put into the company's reserves.

Outside insurance, opportunities for actuaries include working for consultancies that advise companies on employee benefits and the level of contributions they should be making to their pension plans. Actuaries also advise institutional investors in the City of London or working for the Government, providing vital information on pensions and benefits for use when formulating policy. Some of the UK's largest corporations have actuaries to look after their company pension schemes, with funds running into hundreds of millions of pounds.

Qualifying as an actuary is hard work: it can take three to six years, during which you will have to work *and* sit some testing examinations, although some study leave is generally available. A high level of numeracy is required, at least a B in a mathematical subject at A level. Employers usually look for graduates with a 2:1 in a mathematical subject and over 90 per cent of entrants to the profession have a degree, so it is advisable to do one if you can.

There are only about 2,000 qualified actuaries in the UK, all of whom belong to one of two professional bodies: the Institute of Actuaries in London and the Faculty of Actuaries in Edinburgh. Most actuaries are well paid in recognition of their responsibilities and because there is great demand for their skills. A newly qualified actuary working in London can expect a salary of at least £30,000, more senior actuaries £45,000 or more and some top actuaries over £100,000.

---

## Kim Pape

*Age* : **25**
*Job title* : **Trainee actuary**
*Employer* : **Norwich Union**
*Salary* : **£25,000**
*Academic qualifications* : **BSc in maths (1st) and five A levels, in maths, further maths, chemistry, physics and general studies**

'A lot of my time is spent working on a spreadsheet on my computer. We build, amend and use quite complicated models, which give us a feel for how insurance claims will develop in the future. It's predicting what will happen in the future based on what's happened in the past.

'I used to work in pensions two years ago. That's a good place to begin because you find out how the company itself works and get experience of a key aspect of the business. I was calculating funding rates for pension schemes, that is, how much needed to be paid in to secure the desired benefits at retirement. Now I'm in general insurance, and the team I'm in works on the commercial business – that's insurance for businesses. Using a computer, we try to estimate how many claims there will be in the rest of the year and how much they will cost when they are settled. To do that you need to get good data. Because of this I spend a lot of time talking with the computer programmers who provide data from the mainframe computer. With something like employer's liability – things like industrial deafness and asbestosis – there can be ten to fifteen years' data to look back at.

'You've got to be able to communicate well because so much of what we do relies on getting information and data from other people. You have to be able to persuade them to provide you with what you need so you can meet your deadline.

'It's not just a nine-to-five job, though. When I get home I have to study. Norwich Union gives a generous study package, which includes forty-five days' leave a year as well as tuition materials, tutorials and residential courses. The exams are tough – not many people pass them all first time. And it's a bit of a shock to fail one when you've never failed an exam before.

'I enjoy my job because, although some of the work is routine, there's always the challenge of the future. In the short-term this means developing new financial models, getting better-quality data and producing more accurate answers. In the longer term, who knows?'

## Underwriter

The fundamental concept behind insurance is that you have to pay more for cover if what you are insuring is at significant risk. In other words, the more likely it is that a claim will be made, the higher the premium. That is why young drivers, who statistically speaking are in a high-risk category so far as the likelihood of being involved in a crash is concerned, have to pay more for their car insurance than experienced drivers with unblemished records. And why, all other things being equal, smokers have to pay higher life-assurance premiums than non-smokers.

It is the underwriter's job to examine individual applications for insurance cover, assess whether they offer an acceptable risk and, if so, what premium should be paid and under what terms. They read through what is known as the proposal form for details, checking to see whether there is a higher or lower than normal degree of risk, then analyse market and other statistical data to get a broader picture against which to set individual proposals.

Increased competition among insurers has meant that in some cases the activities of an underwriter have been extended to encompass a 'go-getting' business-development role. This entails trying to generate business through the intermediaries such as brokers or independent financial advisers who sell the insurance company's products. At heart, this is a selling job and, to do it effectively, you have to be able to spot opportunities and build good relationships with the intermediaries.

School-leavers working as assistant underwriters will probably be paid under £10,000. Graduate trainees will be paid more. Senior underwriters may earn £15–25,000.

---

## Sue Cossey

*Age* : **36**
*Job title* : **Chief supervisor**
*Employer* : **Axa Equity & Law**
*Salary* : **£25,000**
*Academic qualifications* : **BSc in maths (3rd), an MA in maths and three A levels, in maths, further maths and chemistry**

'I started in the High Wycombe office of the company as a graduate working out the surrender value of policies – how much people get when they cash them in. Then I moved to the actuarial department in a supervisory capacity, although I'm not an actuary: I was doing the Chartered Insurance Institute exams from the start.

'I'm now at the Coventry office. When I first went there I was doing quotations on pensions and then helped develop a computer system for the pension department. Now I'm in underwriting. It's a lovely job but there's an awful lot involved. I report to the chief underwriter, who is in overall charge of strategy and underwriting practice. I have a team of twelve, including three supervisors.

'I specialize in life underwriting, which includes disability and serious illness cover. I'm on the technical side, setting guidelines rather than doing any underwriting myself. We meet with the senior underwriters in the life area once a fortnight. We report any problems and they give us market information and let us know what's upsetting the intermediaries. I also have some involvement with the development of new products from an underwriting standpoint. And I talk through policies with financial advisers to help explain them.

'Although I'm an underwriter I do have input on claims, from a medical point of view. Sometimes I have to decide what investigations to do. You need a claims manager's nose to sniff out the small number of people who claim disability but continue to work. I've had to learn about the impact of medical conditions on long-term insurance. I'm a fellow of the Chartered Insurance Institute and I have a diploma in medical underwriting.

'Life underwriting comes down to, has this person got anything wrong with them, if so will it kill him or her? Sometimes you find yourself taking a bit of a gloomy view and you can become a bit of a hypochondriac. Especially when two or three death claims come in for people younger than yourself. You have to try and detach yourself from it. On a more positive note, I do enjoy the variety and the feeling that you are helping people.'

## Claims

An insurance company's claims department settles the claims people make on their insurance policies. That can be anything from a factory burning down to domestic burglary or damage to motor vehicles. As the people claiming have often been on the receiving end of something unpleasant, such as a loss or accident, they are often distressed, so to work in claims you need to be sympathetic and understanding to safeguard the reputation of the insurance company.

You respond to claims either on the phone or in writing, so good communication skills are vital. You also need to develop a sense for when a claim may be fraudulent: if uncertainty or suspicion falls on a claim it will be investigated to verify or disprove it.

Some claims investigators visit area offices to discuss cases with staff or local brokers. They may go to the scene of an accident, interview witnesses and sometimes even visit customers in their homes to discuss claims and make sure that fair settlement is made. They might also give advice on replacing lost or damaged items. If they think the customer's claim is not *bona fide* and that the insurance company should not pay out, they may have to go to court. They are sometimes known as outdoor specialists. Most are given a particular geographical patch to cover and their salaries are £15–25,000, plus a car.

Senior claims handlers may earn up to £15,000, claims supervisors about £19,000.

## Loss Adjuster

Loss adjusters are independent firms that help to settle insurance claims. They visit the scene of an incident, such as a fire, that has led an insured party to make a claim, and help to work out how much compensation the claimant should receive. Loss adjusters generally work on behalf of the insurer but act as an impartial intermediary. They gather details and then prepare a report for the insurer.

As a loss adjuster you will have to deal with claimants who may be shocked and upset after having seen their property damaged or destroyed. Consequently, you need to be able to soothe them and show them you are there to help. You should be observant and have good negotiating skills. Part of your job is to determine what is needed to settle a claim amicably.

There are few opportunities for going straight into loss adjusting. Most loss adjusters come into it after a few years in areas such as surveying, engineering, accountancy or working in claims for an insurance company. To become a chartered loss adjuster – a title recognized and respected throughout the industry – you have to pass the examinations of the Chartered Institute of Loss Adjusters (CILA).

## Processing

Even though computerisation has done away with a lot of paperwork, a large amount of administrative processing still has to be done at insurance companies, much of it, regrettably, pretty tedious. One of the main processing tasks is inputting information from proposal forms, which give details of what an applicant would like insured. Needless to say, keyboard skills are highly desirable for this work.

Other kinds of processing include the renewal of policies, collection of monies owing on them, answering telephone queries and giving quotes on premiums within approved bands. Although processing is not a job that will set the world on fire, it is a good way into the industry for school-leavers: at many insurance companies it offers the chance to progress into a junior managerial position or eventually to move across into junior underwriting or claims jobs, which offer better opportunities for progressing up the career ladder. Starting salaries may be as low as £7,000 or less.

## Reinsurance

The concept of insurers insuring themselves may, at first glance, seem bizarre, but it is an essential part of the industry that allows the original insurer to spread its risk by taking out insurance of its own among a number of other companies. This process is known as reinsurance. In this way the world's major risks can be accepted and spread throughout international insurance markets. Reinsurance companies are, perhaps, best known for providing cover for insurers as protection against disasters such as earthquakes, major fires, floods, hurricanes, oil spills and other catastrophes. They may also reinsure parcels of life policies, or even a single life policy if the beneficiaries stand to gain a very substantial amount.

As with the composite insurers, reinsurance companies employ actuaries and underwriters. There are career opportunities, albeit not nearly as many as with the less specialist life and general insurers, because the number of people employed in reinsurance is relatively low. Mercantile & General, the largest British-owned reinsurance company, employs only about 600 staff. Reinsurance is very much a global business: the world's biggest reinsurers are Munich Re and Swiss Re. Foreign languages are, of course, a great help if you want a job in this field.

## Direct Sales Executives

Some of the insurance companies have direct-sales teams or tied agents whose job is to sell their products straight to the public or to corporate customers. The life part of this business – pensions, life assurance, savings and investments, and endowment mortgage plans – still has a rather dubious image. The direct-sales tactics of a handful of insurers have come in for heavy criticism, proving that there is more than a grain of truth in the perception of salespersons as over-persistent, 'foot-in-the-door' sharks.

This is by no means true of all direct-sales operations, and many involved find it a satisfying career. However, it is for those who enjoy closing deals, and as such does not appeal to everyone; there is quite a high fall-out rate at the training stage as many people discover sales is not for them. You need to be persuasive, convincing, good at communicating with people face-to-face and striking up a rapport. You will also have to learn the ins and outs of financial products and be comfortable explaining them. Moreover, you will have to overcome any resistance the customer has to buying the product. Established sales people get most of their business from referrals rather than cold calling, so you will also need a knack for generating new leads.

The slightly tarnished reputation of direct sales has occasioned the Personal Investment Authority (PIA), the regulatory body, to become more stringent on the training and competence of those working in sales. This in turn has led the insurance companies to seek sales people of a higher calibre. While no minimum academic standard has been set, insurers are increasingly looking to hire those with A levels or degrees.

Levels of pay differ widely, with some companies offering a low basic salary plus a high rate of commission and others a higher basic but lower commission. If you have an aptitude for the work you may quickly be able to earn £17–22,000. Average earnings are in the high £20,000s. But those who really work at it may make £40–50,000. A handful earn over £100,000.

---

## Beverley Loggia

*Age* : **31**
*Job title* : **Senior financial planning consultant**
*Employer* : **Self-employed (but contracted to Allied Dunbar Assurance)**
*Salary* : **Over £48,000**
*Academic qualifications* : **BA (Hons) in aesthetics**

'Allied Dunbar has a whole range of unit-linked products like life assurance, pensions, PEPs. In each case we tailor a solution to suit the individual. No matter who I talk to I know I can help them.

'I've been in financial services since 1987 but I've only been working for Allied Dunbar since July 1995. I was the youngest woman to be a regional manager at my previous company, where, when I was twenty-nine, I was in charge of twenty reps. I'm proud that I made it into senior management but I spent a lot of time there dealing with compliance issues and missed having client contact. So when Allied Dunbar approached me to take over the client bank of someone who was retiring I jumped at the chance.

'I like to sit in with two clients a day – half the time clients come to my office, the other half I go and see them. At a first meeting I find out what they're looking to achieve. Then it's down to me to find the most effective way for them to do it. I get a big kick out of seeing what I do take effect, when people see their financial dreams realized.

'I'm a big socializer. I really like going out and meeting people. Often, contact with a client goes from being a working relationship to a friendship. Then there's more to the job than just being a financial adviser.

'Most of my work comes from recommendations and referrals. If you do a good job for somebody they'll remember you. It's not a business to be in for a short-term kill. You must be ethical and honest. You've also got to have enthusiasm and perseverance to cope with rejection.

'It's not a nine-to-five job and you've got to be prepared to do work for clients that doesn't pay. I have help from an assistant who does the admin and filing and is qualified to talk to clients about certain aspects of the work.

'I think women coming into financial services have the potential to be very, very good because they often have an emotive rather than a monetary response to situations. They can empathize with people. Mine's a lovely job and I'd recommend it. But you've got to be self-motivated. The amount you earn is related to the amount of work you do.'

## Independent Financial Adviser

An independent financial adviser (IFA) is so called because they work independently of any insurance company so that they can give objective financial advice. They are free to sell the products of any insurer to their clients. In fact, their job is to find the most appropriate financial products for their clients' needs.

IFAs don't charge their clients for consultations: they make their money from commission on the products they sell so they have to balance acting in their clients' best interests with selling to them. To do this they have to get as much information on their prospective clients as they can. What is their income? Their current personal situation? Future plans? What financial provisions have they made? Once they have all the necessary information, they recommend the product they believe will be the best choice for that person. To do this they keep abreast of the latest products on the market and the stability of the companies providing them. IFAs sell investment products, pensions and life or health assurance.

To be a good IFA you must be approachable, trustworthy and good at developing business relationships with clients. You also need to be flexible. You have to see your prospects and clients when it suits them rather than when it suits you, which can mean working in the evenings or even at weekends. It is a competitive field in which you face competition from other IFAs, from the banks and building societies that sell products through their branches, and from the insurance companies with their own direct-sales teams.

Many IFAs are self-employed; some work in partnerships with one or two colleagues and others work for small firms. The key to success is to generate extra business from existing clients and to get your clients to refer new prospects to you. During the first few years, making a living as an IFA can be hard, but the best can make over £100,000 a year. Typical income for established IFAs is £20–60,000.

It is a recently introduced requirement of the PIA that IFAs have professional qualifications to demonstrate 'minimum competency', which means that those wanting to become IFAs must hold the Financial Planning Certificate (FPC) set by the Chartered Insurance Institute (CII) (see p. 110, Qualifications).

## Christine O'Mahony

*Age* : **27**
*Job title* : **Independent financial consultant**
*Employer* : **Self-employed**
*Salary* : **£50,000**
*Academic qualifications* : **Four O levels**

'My job is to advise people on how to use their money more tax-effectively. The people I see have usually been recommended by existing clients. I talk to them to find out where they stand financially.

'At a first meeting I find out details such as their income, outgoings and when they want to retire, whether they're in a company pension plan or not, and if not why not. It's a question of planning their finances to help them achieve their objectives. I don't do business at a first meeting but I give them a business card and hopefully they leave with a clearer idea of what they should be doing.

'I don't charge for a consultation. I make my money from commission on the business I write – things like life assurance and pension plans. I have to give my clients fair advice and I'm always proud when I know I've done a good job for them.

'I got into this when I was backpacking in Australia, needed some money and answered an ad in a newspaper. When I came back to England I decided to give it a year to see if it was worth staying in financial services.

'I'm totally independent but belong to a network called Financial Options that looks after training and compliance in return for a fee. Every time I write a piece of business they check that I've given best advice. I have the Financial Planning Certificate series one, two and three which the industry insists that you have. I go to training days where, say, Allied Dunbar takes a group of us through a new product, and sometimes I have meetings with other financial consultants where we talk about new life assurance or other products.

'It's hard getting started. In my first year I made about £7,000, and you wouldn't believe the amount of work I put in just to make that. But now I earn more than I think I'd be able to earn doing anything else. So I'd wholeheartedly recommend it. And I couldn't go back to working for someone else after being self-employed for five years.

'I'd advise anyone interested in doing the same thing to join a reputable company that will train you and take your career forward. It's important to learn about the products as opposed to just getting on the phone and selling.'

## Broker

Insurance brokers, like IFAs, are intermediaries. The difference is that while IFAs deal with financial services products, such as life assurance and pensions, brokers generally deal with risk to property – buildings, ships or cars. Brokers provide the interface between the buyers and sellers of insurance. Their job is to get the best insurance cover for their clients, the buyers of insurance, who may be either individuals or corporations. Brokers vary in size from small high-street firms to multinational concerns. Sedgwick, one of the largest, employs 15,000 people at 260 offices in 60 countries.

A broker works with their clients to find the most efficient and cost-effective way of protecting their assets. As a broker you have to demonstrate to your clients that your advice is impartial and that you are getting them the best deal available. In the case of corporate broking, you have to learn about the business needs of your clients to get them the most appropriate insurance: you have to identify and assess which risks need to be covered and how. Brokers don't assume these risks themselves, they find an insurer to take them on. In some cases this involves negotiating cover at the Lloyd's of London insurance market.

Some of the bigger broking firms have specialist new-business executives, whose job is to generate work from new clients. Also it

**Lloyd's of London**

- Lloyd's of London is the world's oldest insurance market. It traces its roots back over 300 years to a London coffee house owned by an Edward Lloyd. Here, in the 1680s, shipowners and merchants met to arrange maritime insurance. Today it is Britain's premier insurance market and occupies a prominent hi-tech building in the City of London designed by Sir Richard Rogers.

- In the early 1990s its image suffered a knock due to a series of huge losses caused by claims on natural disasters such as hurricanes and earthquakes. It remains, however, a vital institution. It is still the leading international centre for maritime and aviation insurance – but almost anything can be insured on the market.

- Wealthy individual members of Lloyd's, known as Names, form themselves into syndicates to underwrite insurance risks and pledge their entire personal fortunes to meet policyholders' valid claims, which is why some have been financially ruined by the big claims of recent years. There has been much controversy and legal action over the handling of some syndicates.

- Since January 1994 corporate capital (that is, investment companies) has also been allowed to underwrite risk on the market.

- Working underwriters, who are Lloyd's professionals, accept insurance risks on behalf of the members of their syndicates. They negotiate face-to-face with accredited Lloyd's brokers in 'boxes' on the floor of the market. The brokers seek to place insurance risks with syndicates on behalf of their clients. About 5,000 brokers come into the Lloyd's building every day.

- An underwriter's signature on a broker's slip is completely binding. The Lloyd's motto is *uberrima fides* – in utmost good faith.

- The market is run by the Council of Lloyd's.

is common for people to specialize in certain types of broking rather than working as all-rounders. The larger firms are arranged in departments.

Brokers need to be flexible and good at establishing and maintaining fruitful working relationships with clients. The large multinational brokers usually prefer to recruit graduates with at least a 2:1, and language skills are becoming ever more important. Only individuals or businesses registered with the Insurance Brokers Registration Council (IBRC) may call themselves brokers. A broker outside London with a few years' experience may earn £15–20,000; the big London-based brokers will pay more. Senior brokers can earn £50,000 or over.

## Getting In and Getting Ahead

Breaking into insurance now is undoubtedly harder than it was at the tail-end of the 1980s boom. The insurance companies are recruiting fewer junior staff but, if you have sufficient determination, you should be able to land that all-important first job. It remains a merit-based industry. There are opportunities for committed and able GCSE and A-level school-leavers to make it to the top. That said, academic attainment is becoming increasingly important. Most insurers now look for good passes in GCSE English and maths for even their most junior jobs, and the more qualifications you have the better. Generally graduates make it more quickly into senior positions than non-graduates.

At the same time professional qualifications are becoming more widespread and valued than ever before. Industry bodies, employers and regulators are all placing growing emphasis on them as evidence of competence. If you are serious about moving up the career ladder in insurance, you should reconcile yourself to studying for some professional qualifications. For example, most graduates coming into the industry go on to sit the examinations for the Associateship of the Chartered Insurance Institute (ACII, see

p. 110, Qualifications). Every year about 4,000 candidates register to take them.

The CII produces fact sheets on specific careers and has a network of representatives across the country who can offer careers advice. The Institute also employs a careers-information officer at its London headquarters.

Underwriting and claims are both good areas from which to move into managerial positions and create solid career foundations. So, too, is actuarial work: many actuaries go on to take top jobs. Qualifying as a fellow of either the Institute of Actuaries in London or Faculty of Actuaries in Edinburgh is hard work, but worthwhile. City University in London and Heriot-Watt University in Edinburgh run approved one-year full-time postgraduate courses leading to a diploma in actuarial science, which allows for exemptions from half of the professional examinations. Some firms will sponsor their trainees to take these courses.

Since 1 October 1995 anyone beginning work as a financial adviser is given two years to pass the full Financial Planning Certificate (FPC, see p. 110, Qualifications) and thereby be considered competent. This more stringent regulation of the sector by the PIA means that employers are seeking better-qualified trainees. Although many IFAs are self-employed or work for small companies, most begin their careers at large organizations, which may bear the cost of their training.

# Chapter 5 / **The City**

There is no easy way to define the City of London. It is steeped in history and tradition, but at the same time provides a dynamic environment in which ambitious young people can thrive. It is the home of old institutions, yet makes use of the most up-to-date electronic communications. It is a network of markets used by a global patchwork of investors, speculators, banks and traders. Along with New York and Tokyo, it is one of the world's great financial centres. More than that, it is the ultimate free market, powerful enough to influence government policy. It has a reputation for both fair dealing and greed. Vast, almost inconceivable sums of money change hands there every working day. Assets are bought and sold, ventures are financed, risks are taken. The pressure can be intense. And those who work there are rewarded with salaries and bonuses higher than they would get anywhere else.

The City is as much a state of mind as a physical location. The arrival of modern communications, especially the electronic dealing screen, has meant that many typical City employers, such as investment banks and stockbrokers, no longer need to be based within the confines of London's EC postcodes. Indeed, some are now to be found in Docklands or the West End, although most prefer to remain within the City's traditional boundaries, commonly known as the Square Mile.

Only about 6,000 people live in the Square Mile but more than a quarter of a million work there, roughly half in financial services. There are over 500 foreign banks in the City, more than anywhere else, and London boasts the largest markets in Europe for stocks and shares, futures and options, metals, agricultural commodities and petroleum.

Although London is the leading financial centre in Europe it faces stiff competition, mainly from Frankfurt and Paris, but as English is the language of global finance the City has a distinct advantage over its Continental rivals. By the same token, anyone working in international finance who speaks fluent English has a head start over those who don't, for a career in the City does not necessarily mean working exclusively in London: it might lead to a job in the US, the Far East, Europe or one of the so-called 'emerging markets' like South America.

So what does a career in the City involve? There is a broad range of alternatives: for instance, you could become an investment banker, providing financial advice or raising capital for corporate clients. Or a dealer, spending your time trading shares, bonds, currencies or derivatives. You might opt to become an investment analyst, researching a specific sector in one of the financial markets. Or a fund manager with responsibility for investing other people's money. You may choose, however, to follow one of many other paths.

Some of the large international merchant/investment banks are active in all of the areas outlined above. But other companies specialize in one aspect of finance, for example, stockbrokers.

Jobs like dealing in securities and advising on corporate finance are collectively known as working in the 'front office' because they involve regular contact with clients. Staff in these posts generate income for their employers and are better paid than their counterparts in the 'back office', those in administrative and support roles.

The potential for high pay, responsibility and excitement attached to front-office jobs means that competition for trainee positions is intense. The City banks, fund managers and securities houses receive many times more applications than they have jobs to be filled and can afford to pick the cream of the crop. Many will recruit only graduates who have at least a 2:1 in a numerate subject – maths, economics, finance or physics – or those who have a first in an arts or social-sciences subject bolstered by an MBA or accountancy qualification. Computer literacy and language skills are a further advantage. Even then, they will only take on those graduates who can convince them that they have the capabilities and commitment to succeed in what is a demanding and competitive career. The only exception is in currency and securities trading, where a small number of banks and securities houses will recruit those with A levels. Nevertheless, a degree is preferred.

Gone, for the most part – and good riddance! – are the days when you were virtually guaranteed a job in the Square Mile if you were wearing the appropriate old-school tie – though, of course, it still doesn't hurt to know the right people and have been to one of the top universities. But, in its way, access to the upper echelons of the City remains exclusive. Today, however, it is restricted to those who are both academically accomplished and ambitious.

## Merchant Banking

Merchant banks – some of which style themselves investment banks because of their activities in securities trading and asset management – provide banking advice and services for companies, institutions, wealthy individuals and even governments. Although the majority are diverse groups active in many areas of finance, the kernel of their business remains the provision of banking facilities for their clients.

At its most straightforward, merchant banking centres on lending money to clients. Where this differs from what is done by the high-street banks is in the scale and needs of the borrowers. Loans to large corporations can run into tens and sometimes even hundreds of millions of pounds, and lending of this magnitude is not undertaken lightly.

As far as a bank is concerned, it is vital that it builds up a detailed picture of every one of its clients. It needs to know the risks and strengths of a client's business. Before committing itself to making a loan, a bank will want reassurance that the client is financially sound and will be able to pay back the sum lent plus the interest. This is essential because the collapse of a borrower could

lose a bank large sums of money. Often, a bank will seek to minimize its risk by arranging for a syndicate of other banks to share the
lending. Clients may wish to borrow for a number of reasons: to
help them expand, to make an acquisition or to invest in research
or production. Alternatively, finance may be needed to complete
a management buy-out (where the management of a company
purchases a business from its owners), to lease new equipment, to
purchase property or for a host of other special projects.

Although the banks must have a prudent and considered atti-
tude to lending, it is also important that they make loans – after all,
lending generates revenue. There is keen competition between
them to pick up business from clients by offering the most attractive interest rates. But there is more to it than price alone: a human
element comes into the equation. Clients need to have faith in
their bank's judgement and advice. They want the reassurance
that their business is being handled by a high-quality team. If they
begin to doubt this, the chances are that they will take their business elsewhere. Consequently, banks devote a great deal of effort
to developing their long-term relationships with clients. If you
choose to work on the banking side you will need to be able to establish a rapport with your clients so that you can market the
bank's services effectively.

Lending money is not the only source of banking income. The
City banks also charge fees for structuring complex loans and
advising on debt finance. In the case of the latter this could mean
restructuring a company's debt to save it from collapse.

Merchant bankers sometimes have to work to tight deadlines,
which can involve occasional long days. If you're closing a big deal
the pressure can be quite intense but once it is completed it can be
extremely satisfying to realize that you've helped put together a
profitable transaction for your employer.

To succeed in merchant banking you need to be highly motivated, organized, analytical and numerate. You must develop excellent negotiating skills so that you can devise the best possible deals
for the bank while maintaining the confidence and loyalty of your
clients. You will also be accurate and persistent enough to see your

solutions to a client's needs realized. The basic elements of this are making sure the figures stack up, that there are no legal barriers to your proposals and that the client is prepared to follow your advice.

Recruitment is generally at graduate level. Degrees in numerate/scientific subjects are preferred, although some banks will happily take on arts graduates with an interest in finance to ensure they have balanced teams. Computer skills and fluency in foreign languages are increasingly desirable.

Starting salaries for graduate trainees are in the £20–25,000 band. A commercial banking executive with a few years' experience may earn a salary in the mid £30,000s.

## Corporate Finance

This is the heavyweight, strategic end of investment banking where massive deals are hammered out and high-level advice is given. It is well paid, has a touch of glamour about it and often requires inventive solutions. It is also hard work, with occasionally long hours. Typical clients are multinational companies and governments – the big players.

For the sake of clarification, corporate finance may be broken down into three general categories: mergers, acquisitions and disposals; the raising of long-term capital; and privatizations.

### Mergers, Acquisitions and Disposals

For a variety of reasons – for example, to increase market share or expand into a different business sector – companies often elect to merge with or take over other companies. The matching of a buyer with a target company is frequently the work of an investment bank's corporate finance division. This may involve carrying out research to identify suitable companies and put a value on them. The commercial and financial logic of going ahead with a bid will be examined. If this proves favourable the corporate-finance team make recommendations on timing and, perhaps, the initial approach on a client's behalf. Once the approach has been made, the bank takes part in the negotiations, advises its client on tactics and prepares the appropriate documentation.

In today's global marketplace, many mergers and acquisitions (commonly abbreviated to M&A) are cross-border transactions. For example, an investment bank may act for a UK food group seeking to buy an Italian supermarket chain or *vice versa*. A corporate financier should have an international outlook.

Sometimes the directors of a target company will oppose an offer if they believe it is not in the interests of their company and its shareholders. This is known as a hostile or contested bid. In such cases investment banks are pitted against each other, with the corporate finance team on the target company's side working to fend off the approach or to negotiate better terms.

Corporate finance teams also act for clients intending to sell off subsidiary businesses. In this capacity they will assess a fair value for the business, help the client identify potential buyers and negotiate the terms and conditions of the disposal. On occasion, a bank's advice to a corporate client on maximizing the value of its business will extend to proposing, and helping to implement, a demerger, in which part of a corporation's business is floated off into a separate company. One of the best examples of this occurred several years ago with chemicals giant ICI, which demerged its pharmaceuticals division to form a new company called Zeneca.

## Raising Long-Term Capital

Companies need capital in order to grow, and, if they are serious about expanding and competing, they need access to long-term capital. Depending on their circumstances, they may be able to raise it in other ways than a bank loan. The corporate finance team will advise them on the most appropriate capital structure for their needs and then bring it to fruition. In effect, they are the intermediaries between organizations with money to invest and clients who need capital.

One common method of raising capital is to take a privately owned company public by launching it on the stock market. This is called a flotation. In the run-up to a flotation the corporate finance team works closely with the client and its other relevant advisers such as stockbrokers, lawyers, account-ants and financial PR consultants to make sure that the transi-tion is as smooth as possible and that investors will want to buy shares.

Companies whose equity is already being traded on the stock market clearly require a different solution. One option is for the corporate finance team to arrange a rights issue in which extra capital is raised by selling new shares to the company's existing shareholders. Another approach would be to organize debt finan-cing on the bonds market, or to combine debt and equity in the form of a convertible bond, which, at a fixed point in the future, is turned into shares in the company. There are many potential solu-tions, some of which may be complicated, and part of the corporate finance team's work includes developing sophisticated new financial products to sell to their clients.

When raising long-term capital, clients often ask for tenders and presentations from a selection of investment houses. It is highly competitive.

A closely associated area is venture capital, where the funder, perhaps a bank, acquires an agreed amount of a company's share capital in return for financing its start-up, expansion or develop-ment. Each year, over £1 billion is invested by venture capitalists.


Privatization


During the 1980s, under the premiership of Margaret Thatcher, the Conservatives set about privatization with an almost evan-gelical zeal. Billions of pounds were raised by selling off, to private investors, services and utilities that had been previously owned by the state. British Airways, British Gas and British Telecom are but three examples.

Today, privatization remains a political hot potato, but while the Conservatives and Labour continue to debate the merits of private-sector efficiency versus the benefits of public-sector ownership, it is the investment banks that are at the cutting edge. Now they are applying the experience they have acquired in the UK and elsewhere to a wave of privatizations taking place across the world: France, Germany and Italy are all in the middle of huge privatization programmes, and since the fall of the Iron Curtain myriad opportunities have sprung up in eastern Europe. Then there is the developing world . . .

For a corporate finance team a privatization assignment could mean assisting a government in drawing up its whole privatization policy, or working on the privatization of an individual company. It could also entail advising a corporate client on the purchase of some privatized assets. As you might expect, this kind of work may involve a significant amount of international travel, and sometimes a secondment abroad. However, whether you are working on the business from London or elsewhere it is essential that you develop a good grasp of the local political situation, customs and economic conditions.

Corporate finance is among the toughest and most rewarding jobs in the City. It is a career for high achievers, attracting a large proportion of the brightest and most academically adept graduates, many of whom rise quickly to become divisional directors in their thirties. As it deals with convoluted financial and tax issues, anyone with legal or accountancy qualifications will have an edge over other graduates. In fact, young qualified accountants with about a year's experience at one of the Big Six accountancy firms are particularly sought-after.

The hours are unpredictable and, when putting together something like a privatization or equity issue, possibly long. You will need to be resourceful and determined. Other qualities needed include the ability to ferret out new business opportunities for clients, often a mixture of in-depth research and gut instinct, and the confidence to be able to sell those opportunities to clients in a presentation. You should also be personable enough to build up a strong professional relationship with your clients and – equally important, as you will be part of a team that works closely together – with your colleagues.

Tenacity is a prerequisite, as is adaptability. You will need to be resilient and able to cope with occasional set-backs – for example, when a transaction you've been labouring on for months falls through because the client has changed their mind – and, as much of the business is for multinational or foreign concerns, you must be able to think globally.

Starting salaries for graduate trainees are in the £20–25,000 per annum band. A corporate finance executive will earn £35–60,000, and a head of corporate finance over £100,000. Senior corporate financiers are also in line for substantial performance-related bonuses, often topping up their basic salaries by as much as 70 per cent.

---

## Ros Williams

*Age* : **24**
*Job title* : **Corporate finance analyst**
*Employer* : **Schroders**
*Salary* : **£25,000 basic plus bonus**
*Academic qualifications* : **BSc in economics (2:1) and three A levels, in maths, physics and chemistry**

'When I first joined the corporate finance division I worked on a general UK team. We had ten or fifteen clients from a wide range of sectors to whom we provided financial advice, ranging from public offers and defence work to fund-raising and financial re-structuring. Within the first couple of months I was involved in a ground-breaking deal within the radio sector that ended up in the High Court. That was very exciting.

'You're thrown in at the deep end from day one. You quickly learn from your seniors how to deal with things. But you have to be able to think on your feet. You need to be a team player, happy with numbers and very level-headed. All corporate finance work is client-based, so you have to be presentable and able to communicate with your clients. There will be times when a client rings up and they'll want an answer then and there, and you have to find it pretty fast.

'Now I've moved on to an execution team where we carry out transactions. At the moment I do a lot of research, proof-reading and number-crunching, and I'm constantly learning new skills from the people I'm working with. I like the variety of the job. You never know what's going to happen. I walked in one day last week to find out that a client was the target of a £1 billion hostile bid.

'You have to be incredibly committed. You can expect to work 100-hour weeks once in a while, but it's not always like that. Sometimes the job can be frustrating because you can spend a large amount of time working on deals that never see the light of day, but when you're working on a big public deal that comes off and gets on the front page of the *FT*, you get quite a kick out of that. I can't think of anything else I'd rather do.'

## Credit Analysis

The City banks engaged in commercial lending and corporate finance generally have a credit analysis team whose job it is to look into the risks involved in large or unusual transactions. These bankers must be able to work their way through complex accounts and recommend whether or not a deal should go ahead.

It is a job for graduates, with starting salaries of £15–20,000. Those with four or five years' experience may be paid £28–35,000. Senior credit analysts in their thirties may earn £35–55,000.

## Asset Management

Pension funds, life assurance companies, unit and investment trusts and charities all have large amounts of money to invest. They are seeking high returns, but it is usually just as important for them to safeguard their assets. This is where asset management comes in.

Asset management – also known as fund management or investment management – is the process whereby organizations entrust their money to a bank, specialist fund-management company or an in-house team of their own. That money is then looked after by a fund manager, whose job is to increase the value of the client's assets without putting them in undue danger. This is accomplished by spreading the risk across a portfolio of investments. More often than not, the majority of the portfolio will be made up of shares in blue-chip companies (the UK's leading corporations) balanced with some investment in bonds and, perhaps, property. Some clients also want niche portfolios in specific sectors.

Fund managers need to be good at building up strong working relationships. Not only must they be able to work well with their clients but also with the colleagues on whose research they rely, securities dealers and contacts at the companies in which they purchase shares. A fund manager helps clients to develop strategies that meet their performance and risk objectives, and must be receptive to the advice of investment analysts to get the most accurate information on companies and market sectors.

To be an effective fund manager you will need to acquire a thorough understanding of the international financial markets, and be aware of the wider economic and political picture. You should be able to plan long-term but be adaptable enough to spot potential short-term gains. You will be methodical at research and analysis, and capable of assimilating a large amount of information. On top of all this, you must have the courage of your convictions. Decisions on investing millions are not taken lightly.

Entry is as a graduate trainee with at least a 2:1. At first you will work in research, learning about a specific market sector and studying for your professional qualifications. Eventually, say after eighteen months, you will be given your first portfolio to manage. Sizes vary, but it may be worth as much as £250 million. This will probably seem a terrifyingly large amount of money, but in the early stages of your career you will be under strict supervision.

As you become more experienced you will build up your client base. The funds you manage will get bigger and your clients more demanding. A typical day might see you starting work at 7.30 a.m. in a short meeting with a group of stockbrokers. After that you might check what happens when the Stock Exchange opens for business. Later in the morning you may present some proposals to a client. Perhaps you will have lunch with the finance director of a quoted company. In the afternoon you will read and absorb the latest relevant research or articles in the business press. Any one of these activities may influence you to buy or sell an investment on a client's behalf.

A graduate trainee in asset management will receive a starting salary of £20–25,000. Junior fund managers earn £30–35,000, senior fund managers £40–90,000, and fund management directors £100–155,000, with bonuses adding another 25 per cent or so to their income.

## Rosie Reid

*Age* : **22**
*Job title* : **Fund manager**
*Employer* : **Rothschild Asset Management**
*Salary Range* : **£20–25,000**
*Academic qualifications* : **BSc in maths (2:1) and five A levels, in maths, further maths, physics, chemistry, French/music, plus S level maths**

'Before I left school I decided to work in the City and had various summer jobs while I was at Oxford University. I worked at an actuarial firm and two asset management companies similar to RAM. This experience helped me narrow down my career choices by a process of elimination. An actuarial career would have been an obvious choice for someone with my maths background, but although it is very academic I didn't think it was stretching in other ways. So I decided to give merchant banking a try instead.

'I now work in currency portfolio management. These markets are very mathematical and appealed to me more than equities. But I think it would be quite easy for me to cross over on to the equity side if I want to later in my career.

A typical day starts at 7.45 a.m. and finishes at about 6.30 p.m. I begin by looking at the markets and speaking to brokers. There's a meeting where the analysts report on their markets, and much of the morning is taken up by trading and getting positions in order. It's very important to develop strong links with brokers so that they'll put more effort into providing timely information on market developments. The afternoon is used for client reporting, internal meetings and forecasting. Investment decisions are taken by the whole team, led by the more senior individuals.

'There are so many different aspects to the job that you need to be able to think things through. You need a fundamental interest in making money and a grasp of what makes markets move. And numerical skills are very useful. It's very hard work making sure things are done correctly every day. The hours are long and on top of that you're studying for the IIMR [Institute of Investment Management and Research] qualification at weekends and in the evenings. I wasn't prepared for such a tough time. Despite this, it is all worth it.'

## Research Analysis

An analyst's job is to research the financial status and future prospects of quoted companies. On the basis of that research they recommend to fund managers and stockbrokers whether to buy or sell shares in a particular company. Most analysts specialize in following companies that belong to one sector of the economy; so a retail analyst would follow the progress of companies like Marks & Spencer, Body Shop, Boots and Next.

Analysts produce written reports and briefing notes on companies. These look at a company's track record, its current financial position and likely profitability in the short- and long-term. A report will also include the analyst's profit forecast for the company's next set of results and a recommendation on whether to buy or sell that company's shares – this has to be as accurate as possible as investors will act on an analyst's advice.

To produce research on a company an analyst gathers information from a broad range of sources, starting with its most recent annual reports and any coverage it has received in the national and business press. They will assess its performance against other companies in the same sector and weigh up the potential for the sector as a whole. This involves taking into account any commercial or regulatory barriers that might hamper growth in that industry.

Analysts need to form their own opinions about the capabilities of a company's management, and to do this will visit the companies they follow, examine the way they operate, look at how they are trading and meet the management. They also attend analysts' briefings, at which companies discuss their financial situation and corporate strategy with a group of analysts and meet with industry experts and economists.

Although the majority of analysts concentrate on the performance of companies within a certain sector, some look at the whole spread of public companies and others specialize in areas such as bonds or currencies. Some institutions employ their own analysts, while some of the most influential banks and securities houses extend their research activities to cover the broader economic picture by employing their own in-house economists. Jobs of this kind are few and far between and are open only to outstanding economics graduates.

If you want to be an analyst you have to be good at picking out vital information and working out its financial implications. You need to be diligent and possess an enquiring mind. It is a career for those with an academic nature who are able to present a forceful and considered argument. Clearly, the job requires you to spend a lot of time ploughing through reports, balance sheets and financial statements but you must also be an effective communicator. You have to be able to explain your opinions to dealers, the securities sales team and investors such as fund managers and convince them to act on your recommendations.

A career in investment analysis is restricted to graduates with at least a 2:1. Starting salaries are in the band £18–25,000. Once you begin to make a name for yourself your salary may rise to £40–50,000. The most highly regarded analysts may earn in excess of £100,000.

## Victoria Maxwell-Snape

*Age* : **23**
*Job title* : **European research analyst**
*Employer* : **James Capel & Co**
*Salary* : **£20,000**
*Academic qualifications* : **BSc (Hons) in economics and four A
levels, in economics, maths, physics and general studies**

'My degree at the University of Bath was a four-year sandwich
course. I spent the third year working in London for Reuters, marketing their information systems including dealing screens. When
I was there I got the opportunity to go to a couple of dealing
rooms and have a look around, and I had friends who'd worked for
merchant banks, so I had an idea of what the City was about.
What attracted me about the industry is its variety. It's changing all
the time. It's very dynamic.

'I started at James Capel on 31 August 1994. For the first four
months I was moved around a lot between departments. As it
turned out, it was the best way of meeting people in the company.
Then in January 1995 I joined the European Research department
on a small team covering pulp, paper and packaging. Our job
is to produce research for our clients on the quoted paper and
packaging companies in Europe.

'I go to briefings on those companies' financial results and
attend analysts' briefings. I also go on company visits: as quite a
junior person you get to meet all the senior management at the
companies, like the chairman and chief executive. We cover many
Scandinavian companies and there's a lot of scope to travel.

'Sometimes the deadlines for producing research and briefing
notes can be tight. And fund managers, who are thinking of
buying or selling shares, want to know your opinion. If you've got
a new idea, that's what you want to put across. It's quite a
pressured business. You're always busy but you get a buzz from
that. The hours aren't great. On average I work from 7.30 a.m. to

6.oo p.m. But this is an industry where if you work hard more likely than not you'll be rewarded for it.

'Everyone thinks that as a woman in the City you need to be arrogant and aggressive to compete with the men. But it's not like that. There are more women than you expect. I'd like to stay in research. At the moment I'm learning about an industry and learning how to be an analyst.'

## Sales

The nature of a job in sales varies greatly across the City. In some cases, notably at a handful of the US investment banks, it is typified by an aggressive, go-getting approach to picking up new business but elsewhere the onus is more on nurturing long-term client relationships. This is particularly important when the clients are wealthy individuals rather than corporations and institutions.

At some banks and securities houses, a job in sales is known as marketing or relationship/account management. But, whatever the title, the basic role is to sell products and services to clients. Perhaps the clearest illustration of this is equity sales: here the sales person is the link between the research analyst, trader and client and must familiarize themselves with the clients' investment criteria. Then, when a research analyst makes a recommendation that fits in with a client's needs, it is up to the sales person to convince the client to buy or sell shares in the relevant company. If the client agrees, the sales person instructs the traders to carry out the transaction.

Sales people must be aware of their clients' global requirements to generate a stream of new orders. It is a career that demands both an up-to-date knowledge of the products on offer and strong interpersonal skills. A sales person has to be able to evaluate possible opportunities quickly, understand the reasons behind analysts' recommendations and convey them to investors with succinct clarity.

Because the sales force has to understand the fundamentals

of equity analysis, many banks and securities houses place trainee sales staff in their research department for a year or so. This gives them a grounding in the analysis of companies and how their shares perform. It is only after they have acquired these basic skills that they will be allowed to begin selling to clients.

Equity sales staff frequently visit companies, in the same way that research analysts do. Sometimes they may be accompanied by one of their clients. Depending on the location of their clients and the investments they pick, there is the opportunity for travel. There are, of course, sales staff who specialize in areas other than equities such as derivatives (see page 92).

A talented sales person will make a lot of money for their employer and will be rewarded with large bonuses. As performance-related remuneration is an enticing prospect, it should come as no surprise that sales is one of the most difficult City careers to break into.

In addition to a degree, usually at least a 2:1, you will have to be numerate, charismatic and persuasive. The ability to inspire confidence among your clients and colleagues is a prerequisite. You must also have a competitive instinct and a certain mental toughness. You are judged on the level of business you bring in, and if this is unsatisfactory the chances are that you will be given the push. Due to its pressures and lack of job security, sales is not a career that would suit many people, but if you relish being judged and rewarded on your performance, it might be the one for you.

When recruiting trainee sales staff, employers look for evidence of leadership qualities and personal accomplishments as much as for academic excellence, so stress any worthwhile achievements when applying for a job.

Graduate trainees in sales will earn £18–25,000. A mid-ranking sales person may earn a basic salary of £40–60,000, topped up by bonuses of 20–100 per cent. Senior sales people will earn over £80,000 and in a good year it is possible for the best sales persons in the City to pick up huge bonuses that take their annual income to about £200,000.

## Melanie King

*Age* : **30**
*Job title* : **Marketing manager, global derivatives**
*Employer* : **Standard Chartered Bank**
*Salary* : **£45,000 plus a bonus of 0–100 per cent**
*Academic qualifications* : **BSc in maths (2:2) and four**
**A levels, in pure maths, applied maths, history and computer**
**science**

'I started at Standard Chartered in September 1986 after graduating from Southampton. After a six-week induction course I started off doing a lot of paper-pushing but as it was such a new and exciting environment that didn't make any odds. I was a dealer in the money markets for about three years and then moved over to the foreign-exchange desk for about a year. Then I moved to corporate sales where I was selling purely on the money market and foreign exchange side.

'Derivatives were really taking off and in 1991 I was asked to join the derivatives sales team on the interest rate and foreign exchange markets. In October 1994 I was sent out to India for six months to help sort out the derivatives business there. I was based in Bombay but travelled around a lot. For the first few weeks I thought I'd made the biggest mistake of my life, but after that I settled down and began to really enjoy it.

'Now I'm back in London and my clients are mainly UK institutions. I generally start my day with a meeting with our economists. Then maybe there'll be a conference call with our Singapore office where we'll discuss what's happened in the Asian market overnight. You've got to follow the markets – I've got three screens on my desk. And sometimes there's a lot of pressure when the customer comes on to deal. I could be talking to a customer on one line and a dealer in Singapore at the same time, or shouting across to a dealer in the office.

'I may have lunch with a customer – I go out and meet them a lot. I like that about sales because as a dealer you sit in front of screens and don't move.

'You've got to be a bit thick-skinned to cope with getting the cold shoulder from clients but also because you have to handle the dealing room banter, which can get quite personal. But when it comes down to it, the rewards are there in terms of money and job satisfaction.'

## Dealing

The stereotypical City dealer is a brash young man in stripy shirt and braces earning a huge income by gambling with money that is not his own. As is the case with many stereotypes, there is more than a little truth in it, but the reality is not nearly so simplistic.

Yes, a disproportionately high number of dealers are young men. The consequence is that dealing rooms and trading floors are masculine places. The atmosphere is assertive and boisterous: barbed comments and insulting put-downs are traded as freely as stocks and shares.

Dealing is not a career for the faint-hearted. For a woman to stay the course she will need all the talent of her male colleagues and the self-confidence not to be rattled by the occasional sexist jibe. That's the bad news. The good news is that, here, too, things are changing. In recent years the number of women coming into dealing has grown and a good number have gone on to excel in their careers. Moreover, an awareness of dealing's reputation as a bastion of male boorishness and of the need for a balanced work-force has led many employers to look more positively at applications from women. Another factor helping to level the playing field is the widespread use of multiple-choice aptitude (psychometric) questions and dealing tests. These are used to weed out unsuitable candidates from those who are able to act on their own initiative but aren't reckless, who can withstand pressure and work well in a team.

The image of dealers as impetuous gamblers is flawed, despite one or two highly publicized exceptions. Risks are calculated, and based on financial and economic data and a dealer's assessment of the direction a market is likely to take. Nerves of steel are an asset but probably less so than a good head for figures, common sense and faith in your own judgement.

And what of the huge incomes? Well, it's certainly true for those at the height of their powers and the top of the tree. But getting there is no mean feat. And anyone giving serious consideration to a career as a dealer should bear in mind that it is the antithesis of the secure, undemanding job. You need to be motivated by money. You will be judged on how much of it you make for your employer, and if this is deemed inadequate your services will be dispensed with. It is this combination of competitiveness and uncertainty that discourages many from pursuing a career in dealing. Others rise to the challenge. If you think you have the desire and character to be one of them, you will need to know about the following different kinds of dealing carried out in the City.

## Stockbroking

Stockbrokers buy and sell shares and bonds, collectively called securities, on behalf of their clients or on their own account. In the case of the latter they use their employer's own funds to try to make profits on the stock market. This is known as proprietary trading.

At the smaller stockbroking firms, the job may involve some investment analysis and advising clients on the securities they should buy or sell before carrying out the transaction. At the large investment banks and securities houses, however, the job is predominantly about dealing, which means getting the best possible price for the client, and such stockbrokers are generally called dealers.

Dealing in securities no longer takes place on the floor of the Stock Exchange. Today everything is done electronically. City brokers work at dealing screens in large open-plan offices. They track the movement of the markets on their screens and act if they spot an opportunity or a problem.

Dealers take and execute client orders from the sales team. On other occasions they deal directly with clients. Under Stock Exchange regulations a dealer has to acquire securities for a client at the lowest price available at the time of the transaction; these prices are displayed on the brokers' screens. Once a deal has been struck, its terms are recorded on the electronic dealing system and may be checked at any time.

Some of the most important banks and stockbrokers are registered as market makers, which means that under Stock Exchange rules they are obliged to act as principals and 'make a market' in certain securities, that is, to buy or sell them when asked to do so. Market makers quote two prices: one at which they will buy and one at which they will sell. These prices are displayed on dealers' screens across the world.

Market makers buy securities on their own account with the intention of making a profit by selling them on at a higher price. They deal with institutional investors or other brokers, not private clients. Setting the dealing price of securities is the most momentous aspect of a market maker's work, and carries with it a degree of risk. If the securities they hold fall in value they still have to trade in them and may sustain a loss. Therefore, fixing prices requires thoroughness and care. Market makers have to know about the performance and current status of the companies in whose shares they are trading and any outside political or economic factors that could have an impact on share prices. They keep themselves informed by reading the financial press, poring over research on companies and markets and by talking to analysts and investors. Market makers tend to specialize by sector, for example leisure, engineering or media.

Some stockbrokers also undertake corporate broking: the stockbroking part of corporate finance. This might involve, for example, working alongside investment banks to help implement flotations and privatizations. In this capacity a broker will advise on the timing of an issue and the offer share price.

Dealers and market makers begin their working day early, often holding meetings with analysts at 7.30 a.m. before the stock market opens for business, but they are usually out of the office by 6.00 p.m. Working in a dealing room can be noisy, frenetic and stressful. Much of the day is spent talking to clients, analysts and other brokers on the telephone and conferring with colleagues in the dealing room. The pace can be unrelenting. You need stamina, good communication skills and a quick-witted facility with numbers to respond appropriately to price changes in the market. You also need to be able to work on your own initiative and take responsibility for your own decisions. The best dealers are those who can spot a price anomaly and exploit it immediately.

Many brokers specialize in bonds – securities issued by governments, banks and corporations to raise money. The issuer of the bond pays the investors a fixed rate of interest during the period of what is, in essence, a loan. Bond prices rise and fall as they are bought and sold on the stock market. This means that the profit investors make from buying bonds – the yield – varies, although the rate paid by the issuer stays the same.

It is still occasionally possible to break into dealing after A levels, but most banks and stockbrokers will consider only graduates with a 2:1 or above. The degree subject is often immaterial, although anything encompassing applied mathematics is an advantage – but good maths results at GCSE and A level are very important. Graduate trainees start on salaries of £15–25,000, although some of the US investment banks are prepared to pay a little more to attract candidates they consider outstanding. Once a dealer has at least three years' experience, remuneration can rise dramatically – often inflated by large bonuses. Rewards are based on performance, and many dealers earn £30–80,000. For high fliers the sky is the limit. In good years the most successful are able to earn sums well into six figures – and the small number who make it to the top can count on even more. A head of fixed income (bonds) at one of the bigger banks or securities houses may be able to earn in excess of £300,000 per year.

But be warned. It is not a career noted for job security. Many of the smaller and regional stockbrokers are prepared to nurture their staff but some of the City banks and securities houses, especially some of the large US investment banks, have a hire-and-fire approach to dealers. If you do not perform, the chances are that you will find yourself out of a job. Large salaries and huge bonuses have to be earned.

## History of the Stock Exchange

The London Stock Exchange can trace its origins back to the bustling coffee houses of seventeenth-century London where money was raised or invested through the buying and selling of shares in 'joint-stock' companies. During the eighteenth century, the number of brokers increased steadily and the trading process grew in sophistication. Eventually a subscription room was set up in Threadneedle Street and in 1773 the brokers voted to name it the Stock Exchange. At this time it dealt primarily in government debt.

The Industrial Revolution, with its demands for investment capital to pay for mechanization and new methods of production, powered the growth of the Exchange into the Victorian age and beyond. It continued to develop during the early and mid twentieth century, but in 1979 the abolition of foreign exchange controls made it easier for UK institutions to invest money in overseas securities. Suddenly competition from foreign brokers posed a genuine threat to the member firms of the Stock Exchange. Many UK firms were comparatively small and lacked the necessary capital base to compete with foreign brokers, some of which were capable of trading in large volumes.

It became clear that something had to be done, and in the early 1980s the Government threatened the Exchange with legal action, claiming that some of its rules were unfair and restricted trade. A protracted tussle was avoided when the parties reached an out-of-court agreement: the Government dropped its case, in return for which the Exchange initiated major reforms. These far-reaching reforms came into effect on 27 October 1986 and were known as Big Bang because they led to an explosion of activity in the City and reinforced London's position as the leading financial centre in Europe. The most important changes were:

- For the first time outside corporations could own members of the Exchange. This led to a spree of acquisitions by British and overseas banks and international securities firms. By becoming part of a larger financial group, member companies were able to build and utilize a sizeable capital base.
- All firms became broker-dealers, which meant they could act in two separate ways: first, as agency brokers representing their clients in the market; second, as principals buying and selling shares on their own account for their own profit – or loss. Previously firms had been divided into jobbers and brokers: jobbers were wholesalers of shares, who could not deal directly with investors.
- Firms were able to register as market makers.
- Minimum levels of commission were abolished. Member firms now negotiate their commission rates with clients and compete against one another on charges as well as services.
- Voting rights were transferred from individuals to member firms.
- New technology replaced the traditional methods of dealing on the Exchange floor. An automated price-quotation system was introduced: now, trades are made and followed on computerized dealing screens.

**Facts about the London Stock Exchange**

- The Stock Exchange is the main marketplace where securities are traded.
- It deals in four basic types of securities: shares (equity) issued by UK companies, shares (equity) issued by overseas companies, UK government securities (gilts), and bonds.
- It is a Recognized Investment Exchange (RIE), responsible for the regulation and supervision of the securities marketplace.
- On 19 June 1995 the Stock Exchange launched the Alternative Investment Market, a marketplace for shares in small and growing companies.

- The Stock Exchange has regional offices in Belfast, Birmingham, Leeds, Glasgow and Manchester.

*In the year to 31 March 1995*:
- 222 UK and Irish companies were admitted to the Official List of companies quoted on the Stock Exchange.
- At the year end there were 2,089 listed UK and Irish companies. Their equity capital had a total market value of £788 billion.
- Turnover in UK and Irish equity (that is, the value of shares traded) was £579 billion.
- Over 450 foreign companies have their equity listed on the London Stock Exchange – more than on any other stock exchange in the world. They have a total equity market value of £2,000 billion.
- Total equity turnover was £1,275 billion.
- 1,758 new eurobonds were listed, bringing the total to 4,771.
- Gilts issued totalled £31.7 billion.

## The Foreign Exchange and Money Markets

Dealers in the foreign exchange and money markets need many of the same qualities as their counterparts in securities trading. They should be numerate, quick-thinking and able to take calculated risks. Dealing in these markets, together with derivatives, is categorized as the Treasury function by the banks, institutions and corporations involved.

London is the largest foreign exchange market in the world. About 300 banks in the capital trade in foreign exchange (forex). Turnover in forex in the UK is roughly £200 billion per day. Buying and selling foreign currencies enables companies to pay for goods and services from overseas. Forex trading is also undertaken as a means of managing risk, using liquid assets.

Forex dealers work in dealing rooms and are exposed to the same pressures as securities traders. It is a hectic environment in which you need to retain your concentration for long periods of time. Dealers have to absorb information from several sources at once and are called upon to make rapid decisions. A newcomer's training is likely to involve the use of sophisticated foreign exchange simulator programs.

The banks often use specialist money-broking firms to act as their intermediaries. Money brokers work to match buyers and sellers, and advise their clients, usually the banks, on the state of the market. The banks can be confident about the information they are given because brokers do not deal as principals on their own account. Money brokers work in the foreign exchange and money markets.

The idea of a market in money, as opposed to foreign currency, may sound odd but is logical: it allows banks to borrow large sums of money for short periods, frequently for less than a week, sometimes overnight. This enables the borrowing bank to balance its books and the lending bank to generate interest on its spare cash. Transactions of this type take place in the so-called interbank market.

Other financial instruments traded by money brokers include bills of exchange, certificates of deposit and commercial papers. The UK money market is sometimes referred to as the discount market because of the participation of the discount houses. The most significant of these is Gerrard & National Holdings, which works as an intermediary for the Bank of England in the money markets. Discount houses, which were first established almost 200 years ago, are the main buyers of bills of exchange from the merchant banks. They are not, however, a major source of employment: there are only eight members of the London Discount Market Association. The real opportunities for a career in the money markets are with the banks and brokers.

Once again, landing a job as a trainee in the forex or money markets is, in the main, restricted to graduates with at least a 2:1, with qualifications in maths or a related subject and languages preferred. Starting salaries are £15–25,000, but a skilled forex dealer or money broker with over three years' experience may earn anywhere between £40,000 and £100,000 plus a bonus of 20 to 50 per cent. A tiny number of top managers of forex/money-dealing departments, who are generally in their early forties, can earn £300,000 or more.

## Carolyn Giangrande

*Age* : **35**
*Job title* : **Associate director, currency division**
*Employer* : **Prebon Yamane**
*Salary* : **Up to £100,000**
*Academic qualifications* : **BA(Hons) in Italian and French (2:2), and three A levels, in English, French and history**

'As a money broker I act as an intermediary between banks who are looking to lend and borrow money. They use a broker to help them find funds or make deposits because the broker has unique access to the markets.

'Firstly, we supply the banks with information. I run the Italian lire desk, and because it is such a volatile country I really have to be on top of what is happening both economically and politically. I also use my languages a lot, speaking to contacts overseas and reading the Italian newspapers to find out what's happening on the ground.

'The money markets are built on relationships – it's very much about getting on with people and building those relationships. This means that you need to be fairly extrovert and not mind talking to people you might not know very well. It also means that a lot of entertainment is involved, which does impact on your home life.

'Banks also talk to brokers because it's quicker than ringing round all the other players in the market. Speed is essential – you have to be extremely quick. On a regular basis you have to decide what to do instantaneously. It's a real buzz when the markets are moving and you're doing the business.

'A number of things have changed since I've been in the market. When I started I was the only woman among 450 men. It was difficult to be taken seriously. But having reached associate-director level it proves it can be done. Things have changed a great deal, and for the first time in the City women are not just being accepted but encouraged.

'The level of technology has changed as well. You don't have to be a rocket scientist but familiarity with computers is essential to get the best information out of them for your clients.

'In the short term it's a great career with the opportunity to earn very good money and work in a dynamic environment. There is an emotional cost, however. Office hours are seven to five, on top of which I'm out on business three nights a week. Then there are business trips. I travel to Italy a fair bit but also to Germany, Luxembourg and Austria. That can put strains on your personal life and, in the longer term, it makes motherhood a difficult issue to resolve. Lots of people do this for ten years to earn substantial sums and then go and do something else.'


## Derivatives

The collapse and eventual sale of Barings Bank in 1995 shook the financial community and made headlines around the world. You probably won't need reminding that the bank's downfall was caused by losses of about £800 million sustained by derivatives trader Nick Leeson.

Derivatives is the collective term for futures and options. These are contracts based on an underlying product, which can be anything from shares in a company to government debt or commodities like coffee and sugar. At their most straightforward, derivatives contracts are agreements to buy or sell something on a specified future date. They are traded for a number of reasons: by companies hedging against adverse movements in market prices or exchange and interest rates; or with a view to making a profit on the change in price of an underlying product.

There are five futures and options exchanges in London, the best known and most broad-ranging of which is LIFFE, the London International Financial Futures and Options Exchange, but the number of exchanges is likely to drop to four because, at the time of writing (January 1996), LIFFE is in the middle of merger talks with the London Commodity Exchange.

**The facts of LIFFE**

• LIFFE, pronounced 'life', is short for London International Financial Futures and Options Exchange.

• LIFFE deals in futures and options, financial instruments which are commonly known as 'derivatives' because they are derived from traditional methods of investment. Futures and options contracts are agreements to buy or sell a specific quantity of something at a prearranged date in the future; for example, shares in a company or government debt.

• LIFFE is the leading futures and options market in Europe and the third largest in the world.

• LIFFE offers the widest range of financial futures and options products of any exchange in the world and trades contracts in seven international currencies – sterling, US dollars, yen, Deutschmarks, écus, Italian lire and Swiss francs.

• Most of the business conducted at LIFFE is carried out by a throng of traders in 'pits' on the Exchange floor. Amid scenes of commotion the traders shout and gesticulate at each other to set the prices and quantities of the contracts they are buying or selling. This process is known as open outcry. Traders wear brightly coloured jackets, some with designs not dissimilar to jockeys' silks, so that the bank/securities house they work for is easily identifiable. Trainees wear yellow jackets, LIFFE staff blue.

• Financial institutions use derivatives to manage the risk associated with changes in interest rates and equity prices.

• Over 45 million futures and options contracts were traded during the first four months of 1995, an average daily volume of over 550,000.

• Overnight settlement of futures and options contracts is guaranteed by the London Clearing House, which was set up as far back as 1888 to clear coffee and sugar trades. It registers every deal to ensure smooth trading and to minimize any risks. In effect, it buys every contract sold and then sells it on to the actual buyer.

The other four futures and options exchanges in the City are more specialist than LIFFE. *The London Metal Exchange (LME)* gives investors the opportunity to hedge against fluctuations in the prices of base metals such as aluminium, aluminium alloy, copper, lead, nickel, tin and zinc. Tens of millions of contracts are traded on the LME every year. Exchange turnover exceeded $1 trillion in 1993, equating to about $5 billion per business day.

*The London Commodity Exchange (LCE)* handles soft-commodity futures such as cocoa, robusta coffee (used to make instant), grain, potatoes, barley and raw and white sugar. Some commodities are still traded on the Exchange floor by open outcry, the process whereby dealers shout prices at one another. Each product is traded on a different-coloured carpet for ease of identification. Others are bought and sold on the Exchange's own screen-based trading system, Fast Automated Screen Trading (FAST). The LCE also operates a freight futures market: BIFFEX.

*The International Petroleum Exchange of London (IPE)* is Europe's only energy futures and options market. Set up in 1980, it trades contracts based on products like Brent Crude Oil. Trading is conducted by open outcry in 'pits' on the Exchange floor. In 1993, almost 14 million contracts were traded at IPE.

The City's fifth futures and options market is the appropriately named *London Securities and Derivatives Exchange (OMLX)*. Established in 1989, it specializes in trading futures and options based on Swedish stocks and shares.

### Derivatives Trading

If you're brilliant with figures, long to make pots of money and seek a high-intensity job where decisions concerning millions of pounds have to be made instantaneously, derivatives trading could be the career for you. If it sounds like hell on earth, you're probably in the majority. It is a career suited only to a small proportion of those starting work in the City: those who relish the stresses and thrills of thinking on their feet, who have agile minds and enough drive to turn their dealings in complex financial instruments into whopping profits for their employers. Derivatives traders need a sound grasp of global finance to interpret the fluctuations in international markets, but most specialize in one area, for example, equity options or interest rate futures.

The main derivatives exchange in the UK is LIFFE, where business is carried out using open outcry in trading pits on the floor of the Exchange. It requires a forceful personality and stamina to conduct business amid the mêlée, which is why many of the dealers on the floor are in their twenties.

Dealers may receive instructions from brokers who telephone the order desks adjacent to the trading pits, or they could be involved in proprietary trading on behalf of their employers. Every transaction is relayed to price reporters at computers overlooking the Exchange floor and details are entered into LIFFE's registration system for matching and clearing.

Some of those working in derivatives are involved in developing new products, which demands a first-rate mathematical mind, so much so that the people engaged in it are jokingly called the City's rocket scientists. To join their ranks you will probably need a first-class degree in maths or physics and a PhD. Because the standards are so high there is a shortage of these financial boffins, so the rewards can be astounding. Those able to develop successful derivatives products stand to earn bonuses that may be as much as four or five times their basic salary. For a handful this equates to an income as large as £500,000. But we are talking about just a handful. And only the numerically brilliant need apply.

The Securities and Futures Authority (SFA) is the watchdog responsible for the regulation of companies taking part in derivatives trading. About half of its 1,400 member firms are active in futures and options. If you are a key employee of a member firm you must register individually with the SFA, which assesses your character, reputation, experience and qualifications to determine whether you are a 'fit and proper' person to be working in derivatives. Key employees are company directors, traders and the account executives who give investment advice to clients. A career in derivatives will, in all likelihood, involve working for a bank, securities house or fund manager.

Starting salaries are again in the £15–25,000 band. Salaries for talented, experienced traders inclusive of bonuses range from £50,000 to £170,000. The exceptional can make substantially more.

## Bullion Dealing

This is a small market, in terms of the number of active banks and dealers. Gold, silver, platinum and palladium are bought and sold on dealing screens and their prices rise and fall on the basis of demand.

Bullion dealers need the same sort of qualities as other City dealers but, unlike those practising other types of dealing, many are not graduates. Instead, they have moved into dealing bullion through learning about the market in a bank's back office. The price of gold is fixed twice a day and silver once a day by five banks belonging to the London Bullion Market Association: Deutsche Bank Sharps Pixley, Montagu Precious Metals, NM Rothschild, Republic National Bank of New York and Standard Chartered/Mocatta.

## The Back Office

Every bank and securities house has its non-fee-earning 'back-office' staff who work in support and administration: IT managers, financial controllers, personnel executives and secretaries. Because they do not generate revenue they are not nearly as well paid as those who work in the front office. Nonetheless, support staff in the City are often better paid than they would be if they were doing comparable jobs elsewhere. Some back-office jobs are unique to finance, and settlement is one. This is where the transactions made by the dealers are checked and settled up. It is purely administrative and involves a lot of computer-based work. Settlement is neither high-flying nor glamorous. But it is vital. In the past, staff showing great promise have graduated from jobs of this nature to work in the front office. This happens less often nowadays although there is still the occasional window of opportunity.

Jobs in settlement are open to school-leavers with reasonable GCSEs or A levels, but they are not easy to come by. Among the qualities employers look for are computer skills, numeracy and potential. If you have no relevant experience the best route in is as a junior clerk. The job entails keying in basic data and pays £8–10,000.

From there, if you prove your worth, you can progress to a more demanding job in operations: confirming and reconciling orders and carrying out investigations. Salaries are about £12–15,000 rising to £15–18,000 for more experienced staff. A supervisor in the back office may earn £25–35,000.

There are some opportunities for able staff to move into profit and loss (P&L) jobs, which entail monitoring the trading performance of individual dealers. Because jobs in P&L necessitate working closely with dealers, depending on the policy of the bank or securities house, they can be a springboard to a career in dealing.

Another crucial back-office job is compliance. The compliance team ensure that the front-office staff don't break any laws or regulations, such as a dealer misreporting their position or a fund manager infringing the rules of an investment exchange. Compliance officers monitor and advise on legal and regulatory changes. They liaise with colleagues and external clients to check that they are aware of the latest compliance issues, and investigate and report on any transgressions. Most are qualified accountants or lawyers.

It need hardly be said that a compliance officer has to acquire a thorough understanding of the legal and regulatory framework within which their employers work, but you must also be tenacious and have good interpersonal skills. A compliance manager with five years' experience may earn about £40,000; starting salaries are about half that amount.

In response to the Barings débâcle and other financial disasters, banks and securities houses have tightened up the supervision of their trading activities. Extra weight has been given to risk management, and a greater emphasis has been placed on recruiting graduates for trainee positions. The risk-management team analyses trading transactions to assess the level of risk. Often they will look at complicated new derivatives products to establish how safe they are. It is a job that requires extensive knowledge of financial products and markets, and quite a few senior risk-management positions are held by ex-dealers. Starting salaries for graduate trainees are about £20,000. Senior risk analysts earn £60–120,000.

There are also jobs at the investment exchanges, although they are not big employers. LIFFE, for example, has about 500 employees, the Stock Exchange rather more. One of the key areas at LIFFE is compliance and surveillance. Pit observers, who may be either graduates and/or ex-traders, monitor activity on the floor, report on prices and make sure that dealers have been appropriately registered.

It is not nearly as hard to break into the back office as it is to land a job in the front office, but it is still far from easy and experience is priceless. One of the best ways to acquire this is to apply for some temporary work in the City. Here, the specialist financial recruitment agencies can offer you advice and assistance.

## City Lawyers

Fourteen thousand solicitors practise in the City of London and many of the biggest law firms in the UK are based in the Square Mile. That they are located in the City is no accident for they are an essential element of its financial make-up. City law firms advise the banks and institutions on almost every aspect of their work, from corporate finance to property purchases, taxation, investment product development, shipping, takeover disputes, and banking and loan contracts. At the last count, the top twenty City law firms employed 8,700 fee-earners and had a combined annual turnover of about £1.6 billion.

Many City law firms recruit undergraduates, on the 'milk-round', when they are about to start the third year of their degree course on the basis of their second-year results. They look for a potential 2:1 or better. As well as academic achievement they want candidates to show commitment, team spirit and an interest in business. Although law students predominate, most of the firms like to hire a number of graduates in other subjects for the sake of diversity. Graduates in subjects other than law have to do a one-year conversion course on top of the one-year legal practice course that all prospective solicitors must take. To qualify fully as a solicitor you must work as a trainee at a law firm for two years. This is referred to as a training contract, but is still sometimes known as taking articles.

The City law firms look for people who will be able to understand the commercial as well as the legal implications of a transaction. They want good negotiators, and language skills are increasingly important. As lawyers should be rounded and mature individuals, some firms prefer to take on trainees who have taken time off either before or after university. A career as a City lawyer need not mean working exclusively for the law firms: there are numerous opportunities to work in-house at banks and financial institutions.

Starting salaries are about £17,000, rising to £27,000 when fully qualified. A City lawyer with five or six years' experience can earn £50–60,000. Salary or equity partners at the big firms often earn £100,000 or more.

## Financial Public Relations/Investor Relations

Financial PR consultants work alongside investment bankers, stockbrokers, lawyers and accountants on flotations, privatizations, and mergers and acquisitions. The main thrust of their work, however, is providing corporate clients with financial communications advice and publicizing their annual and interim results through the media.

At least 90 per cent of entrants into financial PR are graduates, although the subject or indeed the class of degree is often of secondary importance. What financial PR consultancies look for is a combination of writing skills, numeracy, the ability to communicate clearly and the mental dexterity to switch in an instant from handling one client to another. To land a job as a graduate trainee you will have to show that you are interested in business and have an understanding of a client's financial communications needs. Fluency in a foreign language also helps.

A significant number of people enter financial PR after spending a couple of years working in banking, accountancy or financial journalism. The knowledge and contacts acquired in such jobs is of value to consultancies, so they will pay newcomers with this sort of experience rather more than graduate trainees. Account handlers at a financial PR consultancy work in teams and usually report to either an account manager or account director.

Salaries for graduate trainees are in the bracket £14–£20,000. Account executives earn £18–25,000, account managers £25–30,000 and account directors £40,000 or more. Salaries for board directors vary markedly depending on the size and success of the consultancy, but at the bigger consultancies some earn over £100,000.

A job in investor relations (IR) usually means working in-house at a large corporation with a brief to protect and enhance the company's reputation among its shareholders and potential investors. In many respects it is a second career as many senior IR practitioners were previously fund managers, research analysts, finance department executives or corporate communications consultants. Experience of finance and investment is a virtual prerequisite for an IR job.

Most senior IR practitioners belong to the Investor Relations Society (IRS), which is useful both for exchanging information and networking.

## Shipbroking (the Baltic Exchange)

Like Lloyd's of London (see Chapter 4 on Insurance), the Baltic Exchange developed from Britain's historic role as an international shipping and trading power. Its origins lie in the Virginia and Maryland coffee house where, in the eighteenth century, shipowners and merchants met to thrash out the import and export costs for consignments of goods.

Today, the Baltic Exchange is the only international shipping exchange in the world. It has nearly 600 member companies on behalf of which about 1,500 individuals are allowed to work as shipbrokers on the Exchange floor. Though shipbrokers do still meet and make contacts at the Exchange, in practice it is more of a club than a market. Most transactions are conducted by telephone or at meetings elsewhere.

The main business of a shipbroker is to match cargoes with available ships across the world at the most favourable price for a client. The types of cargo dealt with include grain, iron ore, coal, bauxite, sugar, wood and fertilizer. London is the leading international market for shipbroking – it is said that about half of the world's open-market bulk-cargo movement is at some stage handled by members of the Baltic Exchange.

Shipbrokers may work in specialist areas such as chartering oil tankers or acting as agents in the buying and selling of ships, known as Sale and Purchase (S&P). Some shipbroking companies also work in airbroking, which, as its name suggests, is the chartering or sale and purchase of aircraft.

Shipbroking is a truly global business, so international travel is part and parcel of the job, but the need to keep in touch with what is going on overseas also means working long hours, sometimes into the night, and being prepared to change your plans at the drop of a hat. If you are looking for a structured, predictable job, then the chances are that shipbroking is not for you.

Qualities needed for the job include flexibility, accuracy, persistence and the ability to get on well with clients. Clinching a deal may be far from straightforward and requires perseverance and negotiating skill. Also, because of the nature of the shipping business, transactions often have to be completed quickly, which may mean that not everything is set down in writing. As a consequence, shipbrokers are expected to have unquestionable integrity. This is reflected in the motto of the Baltic Exchange. 'Our Word, Our Bond'.

A good shipbroker must develop an understanding of the broader economic picture and have the capacity to assimilate detailed information; much of this essential market data is delivered via computer screen.

Unfortunately, jobs in shipbroking are hard to come by: most shipbroking companies are small and at best hire only a handful of trainees a year. Demand for places far outstrips the number of jobs on offer, which means that unless your CV is something special you have to prove yourself single-minded just to get an interview. A director of a shipbrokers' told me that his company's policy was not to reply to a job applicant's first letter; it was only those determined enough to make contact again who were considered worth seeing.

Basic starting salaries are £12–14,000 a year. Junior shipbrokers with a couple of years' experience may earn about £18,000, mid-ranking brokers £25–35,000 and seniors £45–55,000. Brokers are also paid commission on the deals they put together and, in a good year, the best can double their salaries.

## Getting Ahead in the City

There are two main networking organizations for women in the City. The first, Women in Banking and Finance, is open to any woman working in finance. It organizes training courses, lectures, leisure events and introductory drinks evenings for prospective members, and publishes a newsletter for its 200-plus members.

The organization exists to promote the role of women in the banking and finance community. Membership is £30 per annum.

The second, City Women's Network, is open only to women with five years' managerial or professional experience at a senior level. It publishes a monthly newsletter, *Connections*, and its objective is to highlight the contributions women make to the City. It has about 250 members, who exchange views, skills and knowledge, and build professional and personal contacts through the network.

Another solid platform for making contacts and furthering your career is the Securities Institute, which was formed in March 1992 after the London Stock Exchange surrendered its individual membership responsibilities. It is an independent professional body for qualified practitioners of a range of securities and investment business activities. Membership, which is now approaching 10,000, is open to those with at least three years' relevant experience who have passed the Securities Institute Diploma (SID). For those in the early stages of their careers, the Securities Institute offers student membership. In 1994, this had risen by 48 per cent over the previous year. Student members pay a joining fee of £25 and an annual fee of £30. Some employers will happily pay these fees on behalf of their staff (it can't hurt to ask!). Although about two-thirds of its members are in the City of London, the Securities Institute has a regional network of nineteen branches. These, together with its City head office, run a series of social and educational events that are handy for boning up on developments in the industry and meeting people who may one day offer you a job.

The Institute of Investment Management and Research (IIMR) fulfils a similar function for budding fund managers and research analysts, staging a programme of presentations, discussion meetings and seminars that combine professional development with the opportunity to meet the right people.

# Chapter 6 / **Qualifications and Training**

## Professional Qualifications

Accountancy

Five bodies in Britain offer professional accountancy qualifications approved by the Board of Accreditation of Educational Courses (BAEC): the Institute of Chartered Accountants in England and Wales (ICAEW); the Institute of Chartered Accountants of Scotland (ICAS); the Chartered Institute of Management Accountants (CIMA); the Chartered Association of Certified Accountants (ACCA); and the Chartered Institute of Public Finance and Accountancy (CIPFA). A sixth body, the Institute of Chartered Accountants in Ireland (ICAI), works closely with BAEC and its qualifications are widely respected. To become a member of one of these bodies you must pass its examinations and gain a minimum of three years' experience working in accountancy.

The ICAEW is the largest, with over 100,000 members. To become a member of the ICAEW, that is a *chartered accountant*, you must complete a training contract (see Training, p. 114) at an office approved by the Institute, and pass its demanding professional exams. A chartered accountant – that is, a member of the ICAEW or its sister bodies in Scotland and Ireland, ICAS, ICAI – can use the internationally recognized letters ACA after their name.

The majority of ICAEW trainees are graduates with at least a first- or upper-second-class degree, but it is possible for nongraduates to train as chartered accountants. The minimum academic qualifications laid down by the ICAEW are two A levels or equivalent (BTec National/GNVQ level three) plus passes in

GCSE maths and English. It is recommended that candidates have at least three A levels at grade C or above. To qualify, graduates and non-graduates alike must pass the Institute's Intermediate and Final examinations (known until recently as PE1 and PE2). Training for these examinations takes place predominantly at accountancy firms, but since 1993 it has been possible to take the Intermediate examination independently. Some students now choose to pay for and take the exam before starting a training contract, but although some grants are available this is usually expensive and, more to the point, offers no guarantee of employment.

The ACCA qualification for *certified accountants* is similarly broad-based. The main difference from the chartered-accountancy qualification is that it is more geared towards working in commerce and industry. This is because most certified accountants train outside public practice (unlike the majority of chartered accountants). ACCA is also regarded as a sound qualification for management accounting. By law, only chartered and certified accountants are allowed to act as auditors, which, in the UK, means qualifying as an ACCA or ACA.

The CIMA qualification for *management accountants* places even greater emphasis on business organization and control. It is as much a business management qualification as an accountancy one, and the majority of CIMA-qualified accountants work in commerce and industry. That said, a number are also to be found in the public sector or working in management consultancy at the larger accountancy firms.

The CIPFA qualification, meanwhile, is specifically aimed at those planning a career in the *public sector*, such as the civil service or local government, but as the public sector has shrunk in the wake of privatizations and contracting-out of services to the private sector, so the qualification has become more wide-ranging and CIPFA-qualified accountants now work in the private sector too.

The *Association of Accountancy Technicians* (AAT) qualification is backed by the five BAEC-approved bodies. It is a non-professional qualification, aimed primarily at support staff wishing to move into a middle-management role. It consists of foundation, intermediate and technician levels (NVQ levels two to four). Certificates are awarded for the successful completion of each stage on the basis of central assessment by the AAT and devolved assessment by an approved training centre. A list of approved centres is available from the AAT.

The AAT is a genuine back-door route into a career in accountancy. It is a godsend for those who don't have the academic record to make it into accountancy in the normal way or who prefer to begin working straight after A levels. Those working in a junior capacity in an accounts department or other financial area will be sponsored by their employers to study for the qualification. It is possible to enrol, even if you're not working in an accounting capacity – though please remember that to qualify for membership of the AAT you need a minimum of a year's full-time approved work experience in accounting.

Once they begin to study, people who had never seriously considered accountancy as a career option can discover a taste and aptitude for the work. The chartered bodies recognize the AAT as an accounting qualification in its own right, and those who obtain a credit or distinction may be encouraged to go on and train as professional accountants. About one in five of those who take the AAT do so. The AAT is the only professional body to offer NVQs in accounting.

The recognized *tax* qualifications are awarded by the Association of Taxation Technicians (ATT) and the Institute of Taxation (ATII). The former is often taken after a little more than a year working in tax, with the latter taken twelve to eighteen months after that. For *insolvency practitioners* the important qualification is issued by the Joint Insolvency Examining Board (JIEB).

The key qualifications for accountants seeking to build a career in *treasury* are acquired through the Association of Corporate Treasurers (ACT). Qualified accountants may be exempt from taking up to four of the six papers in the part one examination for associate membership. There are no exemptions from part two, which is targeted at those on course to move into the higher levels of financial management. It is equivalent to an MBA. Those studying for ACT are generally in their late twenties or early thirties. Most already have an accountancy qualification and a degree.

## Banking

The Chartered Institute of Bankers (CIB), one of the oldest and largest professional bodies in the world, offers a number of vocational qualifications for those working in banks or building societies. The *Certificate in Financial Services Practice* (CFSP) is designed for customer service staff. No entry qualifications are required. Candidates build their own study programme from a range of modules with study support available through the CIB. Holders of the certificate may progress to the final stage of the Banking Certificate.

The *Certificate for Financial Advisers* (CeFA), was introduced in 1995 to meet the tightened regulatory requirements of the Personal Investment Authority (PIA) and Investment Management Regulatory Organization (IMRO) and is now an integral part of the CIB's qualifications structure. CeFA is aimed at bank staff who will be advising on and selling financial products such as life assurance, mortgages, PEPs, unit trusts and various other investments. The examination consists of three papers, Introduction to Financial Services and Products, Financial Products, and Client Assessment and Advice. The first two papers are intended to give candidates the knowledge and understanding they need to work as financial advisers; the third tests their ability to apply this knowledge.

The *Banking Certificate* is a three-year course aimed at those who hope to reach a senior supervisory level. Successful candidates may use the recognized designatory letters Cert. CIB after their names. The one-year preliminary section is open to all and is the basis for further study. Candidates with one or more A levels and GCSE English language grade C or above, or, more rarely, five years' relevant work experience, may enter the final section direct.

For anyone aspiring to management, the key qualification is the

*Associateship of the Chartered Institute of Bankers.* The examinations usually take about three years of part-time study to complete. To be awarded the Associateship you must pass the exams, have three years' banking experience and have been a member of the CIB for three years. To enter you must have either a recognized degree or professional qualification or the Banking, Certificate. Alternatively, you can follow the *Pre-Associateship Route*, which is a fast track to entry for students with at least one A level and GCSE English language grade A–C. This is, however, not a qualification in its own right so many candidates prefer to study for the final section of the Banking Certificate instead. Candidates for the Pre-Associateship route must pass the four subjects on which they are tested within a maximum of three consecutive attempts.

Another recent addition to the CIB's stable of qualifications is the *Diploma in Mortgage Lending*. This is a 'free-standing' qualification, developed in association with the Council of Mortgage Lenders, designed to meet the needs of specialist staff working for building societies and other mortgage lenders. Although the diploma has merit in its own right it is also a pathway to Associateship of the CIB: passes gained studying for the diploma are also credited as Associateship paper passes for those candidates who go on to study for the ACIB qualification. Candidates must pass three papers to be awarded the diploma. This includes one compulsory subject: Residential Lending and Property Law.

CIB Associates aiming to move up into senior management may wish to take part in the *Lombard Scheme*, a programme leading to the award of a master's degree in business administration (MBA) for those in banking and finance. This requires genuine commitment, between nine and fifteen hours' study a week in addition to classes. It may also be costly, although over half of all Lombard Scheme students receive financial assistance from their employers. The Lombard MBA course includes banking electives, scheduled towards the end of the programme. On successful completion students receive a financial-studies diploma and may use the designatory letters Dip.FS.

The Chartered Institute of Bankers in Scotland has its own set of qualifications, some of which are comparable to those of the CIB. Its *Certificate in Financial Services* is of a standard roughly half-way between the CIB's Certificate in Financial Services Practice and its Banking Certificate. The *Certificate in Investment Planning* is the Scottish equivalent of CeFA. The Scottish Institute also has its own *Associateship* qualification, holders of which may put the letters ACIBS after their names. There is also a special Associateship qualification developed jointly with the British Computer Society for those working in information technology within banking. The designatory letters for this qualification are ACIBS (IT). Finally, there is *Membership* of the CIBS, a higher qualification open to Associates of the Institute, which is pitched close to MBA level.

For a career in *factoring* the key qualifications are the *Certificate* and *Diploma* offered by the Association of British Factors and Discounters. Both are obtained by examination; the diploma is the higher-level qualification.

## Insurance and Personal Finance

The Chartered Insurance Institute (CII) offers correspondence courses for a number of widely recognized qualifications that can play an important part in your career development. No minimum academic standards are required to enrol for the *Certificate of Proficiency*, which offers a basic introduction to *underwriting*, insurance products and services, *claims* and voluntary and statutory regulation. It is suggested that you allow a total of seventy-five hours' study time to prepare for the two papers.

The *Certificate of Insurance Practice* (CIP) is intended to prove a high level of technical knowledge in a specialist area. To enrol for the CIP you should be twenty-one or over, or have either at least four GCSEs at grade C or above, the CII Certificate of Proficiency or the Financial Planning Certificate (see below). You have to pass five examinations in three subject blocks to get your certificate. That means taking three subjects at foundation level from a choice of four; one subject at branch level, again from a choice of four; and one at specialist level, this time from a choice of thirteen. You should expect to spend a minimum of forty hours in studying for each subject. Passing the CIP qualifies you for membership of the Society of Technicians in Insurance and allows you to put the letters MSTI after your name.

The *Financial Planning Certificate* (FPC) is one of the benchmark qualifications for *financial advisers*, who sell and advise on savings and investment products. It marks the 'minimum competence' for those involved in financial planning and is endorsed by the industry regulators. The FPC comprises three papers: Financial Services and their Regulation; Protection, Savings and Investment Products; Identifying and Satisfying Client Needs. You will need to spend between forty and eighty hours in studying for each paper, depending on your experience. Holders of the FPC are eligible to use the description 'certified in financial planning by the Chartered Insurance Institute'.

The other principal qualifications for financial advisers are CeFA (see Banking, p. 107) and the Securities Institute's Investment Advice Certificate (IAC), which is recognized by IMRO, PIA and the Securities and Futures Authority. The IAC is designed for retail-investment advisers who specialize in PEPs, bonds and unit trusts rather than life assurance and pensions. It is made up of three papers: Introduction to Financial Services; Investments, Savings and Protection Products; Financial Advice.

The *Advanced Financial Planning Certificate* (AFPC) is open only to those who already have the FPC or IAC, although associates and fellows of the CII are given some exemptions, as are graduates with approved financial-services degrees. You must take three out of four papers for the AFPC. One paper, Tax and Trusts, is compulsory. The other three are: Personal Investment Planning, Business Financial Planning, and Pensions. The qualification demonstrates a comprehensive knowledge of financial planning and holders are given automatic membership of the Society of Financial Advisers, giving them the right to put the letters MSFA after their names.

Associateship of the CII is internationally recognized, and holders of the qualification can use the letters ACII after their names. ACII is mandatory for Lloyd's underwriters and is becoming a requirement for a growing number of senior insurance posts. To enrol you must be twenty-five or older, or have a degree, GN-VQ/GSVQ level four, the CIP or AFPC. If you don't have the CIP or a relevant first degree, you must pass three core examinations: Risk and Insurance, Contract Law, and Insurance and the Business Environment. You then take seven further examinations (from a broad range of thirty-six options) in the areas in which you intend to specialize; it is recommended that you take at least one management subject. Associates of the CII with three years' further experience of professional practice may apply to become fellows of the Institute. It is the CII's highest qualification, giving holders the right to put the letters FCII after their names. You may also apply to take up the title chartered insurer or chartered insurance practitioner.

To become an *actuary* you must pass two sets of examinations. The first four cover mathematical, statistical and financial techniques and are known as A–D. Many students study for these exams through correspondence courses provided by the Actuarial Education Service. You could also do the one year full-time course run by the City and Heriot-Watt Universities. When you pass, you are awarded the *Certificate of Actuarial Techniques*. The second set of four exams tests the application of actuarial techniques to professional problems. Study is usually by correspondence and takes place predominantly outside office hours, although many employers offer day release for study. Once you have passed the examinations you become an associate of one of the two professional bodies. Finally, there is a ninth exam, the Fellowship paper, which tests critical evaluation and analysis of complex problems, which qualifies you as a fellow of one of the professional bodies.

The City

The key *fund management* qualification is the *Investment Management Certificate Associate* examination, provided by the Institute of

Investment Management and Research (IIMR). The syllabus covers regulatory bodies, legislation, financial instruments, markets, taxation, portfolio management, accounting, economics and statistics.

While studying, you will be classified as a student member of the IIMR. Once you pass and have at least two years' experience you become an associate member of the IIMR. Academic qualifications in fund management are also available: City University Business School, for example, offers an MSc in Investment Management.

To be able to give investment advice on *securities* you need to pass the most relevant to your chosen area of specialization of the *Securities and Futures Authority Registered Persons* examinations, widely referred to as the SFA Registered Reps exams. These are held regularly at the Securities Institute in the City of London, and less frequently at regional centres elsewhere in the UK. The four main categories are: Securities and Financial Derivatives Representative, Securities Representative, Futures and Options Representative, and Corporate Finance Representative. To be allowed to give advice on the full range of financial instruments – equities, interest-rate instruments and derivatives – you must pass the SFA's General Registered Representative examination.

It is possible to enter yourself privately for these qualifications but it is important to note that a pass does not in itself guarantee admission to the SFA's registers. You must be an employee of an SFA member firm to be granted registered-person status. Most employers in the sector pay for their trainee registered reps to go on external courses in preparation for the examinations. The leading specialists in SFA training are BPP Financial Courses (0171–490 4323), Hyperion Training (0171–374 4007), Financial Training (0171–265 1011) and City University Business School (0171–477 8000).

The *Securities Institute Diploma* is not a mandatory qualification, but it is advisable to have it if you are serious about developing your career in the securities sector of the City – not least because, without the diploma, you cannot become a member of the Securities Institute, with the status and networking opportunities that

that affords. For this diploma you must pass examinations in the three categories, out of a total of ten, most relevant to the type of securities and investment work you do in your job. The subject papers are: Regulation and Compliance; Interpretation of Financial Statements; Private Client Investment Advice and Management; Investment Analysis; Financial Futures and Options; Institutional Investment Advice; Fund Management; Bond and Fixed Interest Markets; Corporate Finance; Operations Management. These examinations are intended to ensure high standards of practice within the industry and, as a consequence, are demanding. Candidates are tested on their technical knowledge but are also asked to devise financially sound solutions for day-to-day business problems. Because of its exacting standards, the pass rate for the diploma is only about 50 per cent.

However, the Securities Institute recognizes the qualifications of some other professional bodies as being equivalent – or partially equivalent – to its own, for the purposes of associate membership. For details contact the Securities Institute or the registered persons examinations manager at the SFA.

No specific academic qualifications are required to become a securities dealer – for example, a stockbroker or derivatives trader – but as competition for vacancies is intense the banks and securities houses can afford to be choosy. Most will only take on graduates. In addition, each of the City's investment exchanges has its own mandatory trader-training programme, most of which include examinations (see Training, pp. 116–18).

If you're thinking of working in the *back office*, the key qualification is the *Investment Administration Qualification – Merit Award*. For this you work through a series of modules using self-study books and pass multiple-choice examinations in three subjects. The modules include: Introduction to Securities and Investments: Introduction to Futures and Options; Global Custody.

The majority of graduates starting work as *City lawyers* have taken a law degree, but those with degrees other than law can join the route to qualification as a solicitor by taking the *Common Professional Examination*, a one-year full-time or two-year part-time course. Alternatively, you can take a two-year senior status law degree, or a one-year full-time postgraduate diploma in law. The next step for all prospective solicitors is the *Legal Practice Course*, which can be taken as a full-time course over one year or as a part-time course for two years. Grants are sometimes available, and a number of firms will sponsor students. For detailed information on qualifying as a solicitor, apply to the Law Society.

Educational requirements for *shipbroking* vary from company to company. A degree is preferable but quite a few shipbroking companies will take on school-leavers and put them through their own training schemes. Some employers in the sector encourage their staff to study for qualifications awarded by the Institute of Chartered Shipbrokers. The International Centre for Shipping, Trade and Finance at the City University Business School runs an MSc in Shipping, Trade and Finance. Students applying to join the course are required to hold at least a 2:1 honours degree or an equivalent professional examination. It is preferred that applicants have at least two years' work experience.

## Training

### Accountancy

Professional training contracts run for three years for graduates and four years for non-graduates. Those who have 'relevant' degrees – that is, accountancy – are exempt from the foundation stage. The training is a combination of work experience and studying for the professional examinations. Employers are expected to pay tuition and exam costs and to provide some study leave in the run-up to a candidate's first attempt. Studying is usually done part-time on a 'link' course.

The vast majority of budding chartered accountants train at accountancy firms, but since 1991 it has been possible for prospective ICAEW members to train outside public practice (TOPP) at approved commercial and industrial organizations. Allied Dunbar

Assurance, the Post Office, London Transport, the National Audit Office, Fisons Pharmaceuticals and Woolworth's are among the organizations taking part. TOPP usually involves a three- or four-year training contract, which combines practical, on-the-job experience with formal study, leading to the Institute's professional exams. Further information is available from the student recruitment and promotion section of the Institute.

Almost everyone working for the CIMA qualification trains in commerce and industry, while CIPFA students almost invariably train in the public sector. ACCA students may train in commerce, industry, the public sector or public practice.

Qualified accountants are expected to continue studying and taking training courses throughout their careers as part of their Continuing Professional Development. The ICAEW offers 50 per cent discounts on course fees for women taking a career break.

## The City

The Securities Institute has a training arm which runs regular introductory and advanced courses on securities, investment management and related areas as part of its professional education programme.

A number of bodies run courses on derivatives at either an introductory level or in advanced specialist areas as an addition to the training given by the City's futures and options exchanges. The training arm of the Securities Institute runs introductory courses on derivatives as well as continuation training, which provides updates on important regulatory and market developments. The Futures and Options Association holds a series of seminars and workshops on key issues, and the London Clearing House organizes courses for those involved in back-office work such as settlement, clearing and administration.

## London International Financial Futures and Options Exchange (LIFFE)

To become eligible for the floor-traders' course you must first take a preliminary induction course on the structure and systems of LIFFE and notch up at least a month watching its trading floor in action. There are two stages to the floor-traders' course. The first is theory, which is split into six computer-based training modules, which cover areas such as futures contracts, derivatives terminology and the rules and procedures of the exchange. There is an examination on each module. The second stage is practical. You take three training sessions on the floor of LIFFE, after it has finished trading for the day; then you are tested on what you have learnt. Finally, you are interviewed by a panel, which assesses your suitability to become a trader. Assuming you are successful, you may then begin trading under supervision on the exchange floor. After three months or so you will be interviewed again, and a decision will be taken as to whether you are ready to begin trading unsupervised.

LIFFE also runs a training course on back-office procedures for derivatives, including commodity futures and options. The course is followed by an optional examination, which is useful if you are starting your career in derivatives in a supporting capacity in the back office.

If you are going to work as a trader with the Automated Pit Trading (APT) computer-based system – used after the Exchange floor closes for the day – it is mandatory to receive training in this from LIFFE.

## London Commodity Exchange (LCE)

There are five modules in the LCE training programme, covering a general introduction to the exchange, market rules and regulations, making bids/offers, trading systems and administration. Once you have passed examinations in these you become a 'red badge', which means that you may trade on the floor of the exchange under supervision until you have acquired enough experience to trade unsupervised. However, in light of the LCE's proposed merger with LIFFE, its training procedures may soon be subject to change.

## International Petroleum Exchange (IPE)

To become a trader at the IPE you must register with the exchange training manager and undertake the registered floor-trader qualification programme. This begins with a two-day induction course, followed by a self-study modular trading course. At the end of this you sit three examinations. You then begin three months' trading as a probationer as the prelude to a practical examination. Thereafter, the IPE's Trader Review Panel decides whether or not you are ready to become a fully fledged trader.

The IPE also runs a number of additional training courses, workshops and briefings at introductory, intermediate and advanced levels. Further information can be obtained from the IPE's training manager.

## London Metal Exchange (LME)

To trade on the LME you must first undergo some hands-on training and a 'clerkship'. An oral test and interview follow, after which you begin a period of probationary supervised trading, lasting for at least six months. Another interview with an LME panel follows. If successful, you will become an authorized dealer.

## London Securities and Derivatives Exchange (OMLX)

OMLX runs a training course covering the structure and operation of the exchange, including trading, clearing and administration. Anyone whose job will involve them in using the OMLX electronic-trading system Click must undergo training in this before they are allowed to become an authorized trader.

## College Courses

**University of Aberdeen**
Aberdeen AB9 1FX
Telephone: 01224 273504
Accountancy (MA); Accountancy (MA Joint or Combined Hons). Possible combinations include Accountancy with a foreign language or with Management Studies.

**University of Abertay, Dundee**
40 Bell Street, Dundee DD1 1HG
Telephone: 01382 30800
Accounting (BA/BA Hons); Financial Economics (BA/BA Hons); Accounting (HND).

**University of Wales, Aberystwyth**
Aberystwyth, Dyfed SY23 2AX
Telephone: 01970 622021
Accounting and Finance (BSc Econ. Hons); Accounting and Finance and Economics (BSc Econ. Hons); Accounting and Finance and Law (BSc Econ. Hons); Accounting and Finance with a European Language (BSc Econ. Hons); Accounting and

Finance with Welsh (BSc Econ. Hons); Accounting (BSc Joint Hons) with either Computer Science, Mathematics, Physics, Pure Mathematics or Statistics.

**Anglia Polytechnic University**
East Road, Cambridge CB1 1PT
Telephone: 01223 63271
Business and Finance (HND)

**Askham Bryan College**
Askham Bryan, York YO2 3PR
Telephone: 01904 702121
Business and Finance (HND).

**University College of North Wales, Bangor**
Bangor, Gwynedd, Wales LL57 2DG
Telephone: 01248 351151
Accounting and Finance (BA Hons); Banking, Insurance and Finance (BA Hons); Management with Accounting (BA Hons); Management with Banking, Insurance and Finance (BA Hons).

**Barnsley College**
Church Street, Barnsley s70 2AX
Telephone: 01226 730191
Business and Finance (HND)

**University of Birmingham**
Edgbaston, Birmingham B15 2TT
Telephone: 0121 414 3344
Money, Banking and Finance
(BSocSc); Money, Banking and
Finance with either French, German
or Spanish (BSocSc).

**Blackpool and The Fylde College**
Ashfield Road, Bispham, Blackpool,
Lancashire FY2 0HB
Telephone: 01253 352352
Business and Finance (HND).

**Bournemouth University**
Talbot Campus, Fern Barrow, Poole,
Dorset BH12 5BB
Telephone: 01202 524111
Accounting (BA Hons); Taxation and
Revenue Law (BA Hons).

**Bradford and Ilkley Community College**
Great Horton Road, Bradford, West
Yorkshire BD7 1AY
Telephone: 01274 753026
Business Administration–Accounting
(BA Hons); Business and Finance
(HND).

**University of Brighton**
Mithras House, Lewes Road, Brighton
BN2 4AT
Telephone: 01273 600900
Accounting and Finance (BA/BA
Hons); Accounting and Law (BA/BA
Hons); International Accounting and
Finance (BA/BA Hons); Business and
Finance (HND).

**University of Bristol**
The University, Bristol BS8 1TH
Telephone: 0117 9303030
Economics and Accounting (BSc
Hons); Economics and Accounting
with Study in Continental Europe
(BSc Hons).

**Bristol, University of the West of England**
Frenchay Campus, Coldharbour Lane,
Bristol BS16 1QY
Telephone: 0117 9656261
Accounting and Finance (BA/BA
Hons); Business Studies – Finance
(HND).

**University of Buckingham**
Hunter Street, Buckingham
MK18 1EG
Telephone: 01280 814080
Accounting and Financial
Management (BSc Econ. Hons);
Accounting with Economics (BSc
Econ. Hons); Accounting with
Insurance (BSc Econ. Hons); Financial
Services (BSc Econ. Hons).

**Buckinghamshire College**
Queen Alexandra Road, High
Wycombe, Bucks HP11 2JZ
Telephone: 01494 522141
Business and Finance (HND);
Business and Finance – Travel and
Tourism (HND).

**University of Wales College of Cardiff**
PO Box 494, Cardiff CF1 3YL
Telephone: 01222 874412
Accounting (BSc Hons); Accounting
and Economics (BSc Econ. Hons);
Accounting and Management (BSc
Econ. Hons); Accounting with French,
German, Italian or Spanish (BSc

Hons); Banking and Finance (BSc Econ. Hons); Banking and Finance with French, German, Italian or Spanish (BSc Hons).

## University of Central England in Birmingham

Perry Barr, Birmingham B42 2SU
Telephone: 0121 331 5000
Accountancy (BA Hons); Accountancy, combined with subjects including Banking, Economics and International Finance (BA Hons); Business Administration, combined with Accountancy, Banking or International Finance (BA Hons); Financial Services (BA Hons), four-year sandwich course; Law and Accounting (BA Hons); Business and Finance (HND).

## University of Central Lancashire

Preston, Lancashire PR1 2HE
Telephone: 01772 201201
Accounting (BA/BA Hons); Business and Finance (HND).

## Cheltenham and Gloucester College of Higher Education

PO Box 220, The Park, Cheltenham, Gloucestershire GL50 2QF
Telephone: 01242 532824
Business Studies and Financial Services (BA/BA Hons); Financial Services, with subjects including modern languages, computing and business studies (BA/BA Hons); Business Computer Systems with Financial Services (BSc/BSc Hons).

## City University

Northampton Square, London
EC1V 0HB
Telephone: 0171 477 8000

Actuarial Science (BSc Hons), three-year course but also available as four-year course with study abroad or four-year course with foundation year; Economics–Accountancy (BSc Hons); Statistical Science with Insurance Mathematics (BSc Hons), four-year course with integrated foundation year, or four-year course with study abroad; Insurance and Risk Management (MSc).

## Coventry University

Priory Street, Coventry CV1 5FB
Telephone: 01203 631313
Financial Economics (BSc/BSc Hons); Business and Finance (HND).

## Croydon College

Fairfield, Croydon CR9 1DX
Telephone: 0181 686 5700
Business and Finance (HND).

## De Montfort University (Leicester and Milton Keynes)

The Gateway, Leicester LE1 9BH
Telephone: 0116 2551551
Business and Finance (HND).

## University of Derby

Kedleston Road, Derby DE22 1GB
Telephone: 01332 622222
Accounting (BA Hons); Business and Finance (HND).

## Doncaster College

Waterdale, Doncaster, South Yorkshire
DN1 3EX
Telephone: 01302 322122
Business and Finance (HND)

## University of Dundee

The University, Dundee DD1 4HN
Telephone: 01382 344028
Accountancy (BAcc); Finance

(BFin/BFin Hons); Accountancy with Chemistry, Computer Science or Mathematics (BSc/BSc Hons).

## University of East Anglia
Norwich NR4 7TJ
Telephone: 01603 456161
Accountancy (BSc Hons); Accountancy with Law or with a European Language (BSc Hons); Business Finance and Economics (BSc Hons).

## University of East London
Barking Campus, Longbridge Road, Dagenham, Essex RM8 2AS
Telephone 0181 590 7722
Accounting with Economics, Finance, Information Systems, Law or Mathematics (BA/BA Hons); Business and Finance (HND).

## The University of Edinburgh
The University, Edinburgh EH8 9YL
Telephone: 0131 650 1000
Law and Accountancy (Law LLB); Business Studies and Accounting (BCom Joint Hons).

## The University of Essex
Wivenhoe Park, Colchester CO4 3SQ
Telephone: 01206 873666
Accounting, Finance and Economics (BA Joint Hons); Accounting and Financial Management (BA Hons); Mathematics and Finance (BSc Joint Hons).

## University of Exeter
The University, Exeter, Devon EX4 4QJ
Telephone: 01392 263030
Accountancy Studies (BA Hons); Accountancy with European Study (BA Hons), four-year course.

## Farnborough College of Technology
Boundary Road, Farnborough, Hampshire GU14 6SB
Telephone: 01252 391212
Accounting (BA Hons).

## University of Glamorgan
Treforest, Pontypridd, Mid Glamorgan CF37 1DL
Telephone: 01443 480480
Accounting and Finance (BA); Business and Finance (HND); Business Administration–Accounting and Finance (HND).

## University of Glasgow
65/71 Southpark Avenue, Glasgow G12 8LE
Telephone: 0141 330 5668
Accounting (BAcc).

## Glasgow Caledonian University
City Campus, Cowcaddens Road, Glasgow G4 0BA
Telephone: 0141 331 3000
Accountancy (BA/BA Hons); Financial Services (BA/BA Hons); Accounting (HND); Accountancy and Financial Studies, also available as options for combined-studies programme (BA/BA Hons or BSc/BSc Hons).

## University of Greenwich
Wellington Street, Woolwich, London SE18 6PF
Telephone: 0181 316 8590
Accountancy and Finance (BA/BA Hons); Business Administration–Accounting (BA/BA Hons).

**Halton College**
Kingsway, Widnes, Cheshire WA8 7QQ
Telephone: 0151 423 1391
Business and Finance (HND)

**Heriot-Watt University**
Riccarton, Edinburgh EH1 4AS
Telephone: 0131 449 5111
Accountancy and Finance (BA/BA
Hons); Accountancy and Information
Management (BA Hons);
Accountancy with French, German or
Spanish (BA Hons); Actuarial
Mathematics with Statistics (BSc
Hons).

**University of Hertfordshire**
College Lane, Hatfield, Hertfordshire
AL10 9AB
Telephone: 01707 284000
Accounting (BA/BA Hons);
Accounting and Management
Information Systems (BSc/BSc
Hons).

**The University of Huddersfield**
Queensgate, Huddersfield HD1 3DH
Telephone: 01484 422288
Accountancy Studies (BA/BA Hons);
Management and Accountancy
Studies (BA/BA Hons); Business and
Finance (HND).

**The University of Humberside**
Milner Hall, Cottingham Road, Hull
HU6 7RT
Telephone: 01482 440550
Accountancy and Finance (BA/BA
Hons).

**The University of Kent at
Canterbury**
The University, Canterbury, Kent
CT2 7NZ

Telephone: 01227 764000
Actuarial Science (BSc Hons);
Accounting (BA Hons); Accounting
with Management Science or
Computing (BA Hons); Accounting
with French or German (BA Hons),
four years; Computing and Accounting
(BA Hons).

**Kingston University**
River House, 53–57 High Street,
Kingston upon Thames KT1 1LQ
Telephone: 0181 547 2000
Accounting and Finance (BA Hons);
Accounting and Law (BA Hons);
Business and Finance (HND).

**Lancaster University**
The University, Lancaster LA1 4YW
Telephone: 01524 65201
Accounting–Economics (BA Hons);
Accounting and Finance (BA Hons).

**University of Leeds**
The University, Leeds LS2 9JT
Telephone: 0113 2431751
Accounting and Finance (BA Hons);
Accounting with Computer Science,
Information Systems or Operational
Research (BSc Combined Hons).

**Leeds Metropolitan University**
Calverley Street, Leeds LS1 3HE
Telephone: 0113 2832600
Accounting and Finance (BA/BA
Hons); Business and Finance (HND).

**University of Limerick**
The University, Limerick, Ireland
Telephone: 00353 61333644
Insurance and European Studies (BA);
Law and Accounting (BA); Law and
Insurance Studies (BA).

**University of Liverpool**
The University, PO Box 147, Liverpool
L69 3BX
Telephone: 0151 794 2000
Accounting (BA Hons); Accounting
and Computer Science (BA Joint
Hons).

**Liverpool John Moores University**
4 Rodney Street, Liverpool L3 5UX
Telephone: 0151 231 2121
Accounting and Finance (BA/BA
Hons).

**London Guildhall University**
133 Whitechapel High Street, London
E1 7QA
Telephone: 0171 320 1000
Accountancy (BA/BA Hons);
Financial Economics (BA/BA Hons);
Financial Services (BA/BA Hons);
Insurance Studies (BA/BA Hons).

**London School of Economics and Political Science**
Houghton Street, London WC2A 2AE
Telephone: 0171 405 7686
Accounting and Finance (BSc
Hons/MSc); Actuarial Science (BSc);
Finance and Economics (MSc).

**Loughborough University of Technology**
Loughborough, Leicestershire
LE11 3TU
Telephone: 01509 263171
Business Economics and Finance (BSc
Hons); Economics with Accountancy
(BSc Hons); Accounting and Financial
Management (BSc Hons), four-year
sandwich course; Banking and Finance
(BSc Hons), four-year sandwich course.

**University of Luton**
Park Square, Luton, Bedfordshire
LU1 3JU
Telephone: 01582 34111
Accounting (BA/BA Hons);
Accounting and Finance (BA/BA
Hons); Business and Finance (HND).

**The University of Manchester**
Manchester M13 9PL
Telephone: 0161 275 2077
Accounting and Finance (BA Econ.
Hons); Accounting and Law (BA Joint
Hons), four-year course.

**The Manchester Metropolitan University**
All Saints, Manchester M15 6BH
Telephone: 0161 247 2000
Accounting and Finance (BA/BA
Hons); Accounting and Finance in
Europe (BA/BA Hons), with either
French, German or Spanish; Business
and Finance (HND).

**Matthew Boulton College of Further and Higher Education**
Sherlock Street, Birmingham B5 7DB
Telephone: 0121 446 4545
Business and Finance (HND).

**Middlesex University**
All Saints, White Hart Lane, London
N17 8HR
Telephone: 0181 362 5000
Accounting and Finance (BA/BA
Hons)

**Napier University**
219 Colinton Road, Edinburgh
EH14 1DJ
Telephone: 0131 444 2266
Accounting (BA/BA Hons);
Accounting (Diploma); Financial
Services (BA/BA Hons).

## Nene College

Moulton Park, Northampton NN2 7AL
Telephone: 01604 735500
Accountancy and Finance (BA Hons);
Business and Finance (HND).

## University of Newcastle upon Tyne

Newcastle upon Tyne NE1 7RU
Telephone: 0191 222 6000
Accounting and Law (BA Hons);
Accounting and Computing Science
(BSc Joint Hons); Accounting and
Financial Analysis (BA Hons);
Accounting and Mathematics (BSc
Joint Hons).

## Nescot

Reigate Road, Ewell, Epsom, Surrey
KT17 3DS
Telephone: 0181 394 1731
Management and Financial Services
(BA Hons).

## University of North London

Holloway Road, London N7 8DB
Telephone: 0171 607 2789
Accounting and Finance (BA Hons);
Business and Finance (HND).

## University of Northumbria at Newcastle

Ellison Building, Ellison Place,
Newcastle upon Tyne NE1 8ST
Telephone: 0191 227 4064
Accountancy (BA/BA Hons);
Accounting and Information Systems
(BA/BA Hons); Accounting
(Diploma); Accountancy and Finance
(HND).

## Norwich: City College

Ipswich Road, Norwich, Norfolk
NR2 2LJ

Telephone: 01603 660011
Business and Finance (HND)

## The Nottingham Trent University

Burton Street, Nottingham NG1 4BU
Telephone: 0115 9418418
Accounting and Finance (BA/BA
Hons).

## Oxford Brookes University

Gipsy Lane, Headington, Oxford
OX3 0BP
Telephone: 01865 485942
Accounting and Finance (BA/BA
Hons or BSc/BSc Hons), modular
joint-honours degree to be combined
with another subject.

## University of Paisley

High Street, Paisley, Renfrewshire
PA1 2BE
Telephone: 0141 848 3000
Accounting (BAcc/BAcc Hons).

## University of Plymouth

Drake Circus, Plymouth PL4 8AA
Telephone: 01752 600600
Accounting and Finance (BA Hons);
Business and Finance (HND).

## University of Portsmouth

University House, Winston Churchill
Avenue, Portsmouth PO1 2UP
Telephone: 01705 876543
Accounting (BA Hons); Accounting
and Business Information Systems (BA
Hons); Business and Finance (HND).

## The Queen's University of Belfast

University Road, Belfast BT7 1NN
Telephone: 01232 245133
Accounting (BSc); Accounting with
French or Spanish (BSc); Finance
(BSc), four-year course; Finance with
French or Spanish (BSc), four-year
course.

**University of Reading**
PO Box 217, Reading RG6 2AH
Telephone: 01734 875123
Accounting and Finance (BA
Hons).

**The Robert Gordon University**
Schoolhill, Aberdeen AB9 1FR
Telephone: 01224 262000
Accounting and Finance (BA/BA
Hons).

**University of Salford**
Salford M5 4WT
Telephone: 0161 745 5000
Finance and Accounting (BSc
Hons).

**University College Salford**
Frederick Road, Salford M6 7PU
Telephone: 0161 736 6541
Business and Finance (HND), with
opportunity to specialize in Finance,
Languages in Business, Marketing or
Personnel.

**The University of Sheffield**
Sheffield S10 2TN
Telephone: 01742 768555
Accounting and Financial
Management (BA Hons); Accounting
and Financial Management (BA Dual
Hons), available with Computer
Science, Economics, Information
Management or Mathematics.

**Sheffield Hallam University**
City Campus, Pond Street, Sheffield
S1 1WB
Telephone: 0114 2720911
Accounting and Management Control
(BA Hons); Financial Services (BA
Hons); Business and Finance (HND).

**University of Southampton**
Southampton, Hampshire SO17 1BJ
Telephone: 01703 595000
Business Economics and Accounting
(BSc Joint Hons); Accounting (BSc
Joint Hons), available with Economics,
Finance, Law, French, German,
Portuguese, Spanish or Statistics.

**Southampton Institute of Higher
Education**
East Park Terrace, Southampton,
Hampshire SO9 4WW
Telephone: 01703 319000
Accountancy (BA Hons); Accountancy
and Law (BA Hons); Business and
Finance (HND).

**South Bank University**
Borough Road, London SE1 0AA
Telephone: 0171 928 8989
Accounting and Finance (BA/BA
Hons); Accounting and Computing
(BA/BSc Hons); Accounting and
Mathematics (BA/BSc Hons);
Management and Accounting
(BA/BSc Hons).

**Staffordshire University**
College Road, Stoke on Trent ST4 2DE
Telephone: 01782 744531
Accounting Information Technology
(BA/BA Hons); Accounting and
Finance (BA/BA Hons).

**The University of Stirling**
The University, Stirling FK9 4LA
Telephone: 01786 473171
Accountancy (BAcc/BAcc Hons);
Business Studies–Financial Studies
(BA/BA Hons); Financial Studies
(BA/BA Hons); Financial Studies
(BA/BA Hons), with Business Law,
Computing Science, French, German,

Japanese, Management Science, Marketing, Mathematics, Spanish or Sports Studies; Accountancy (BAcc/BAcc Hons), with options as per Financial Studies above.

### The University of Strathclyde
Glasgow G1 1XQ
Telephone: 0141 553 4170
Accounting and Technology (BSc Hons).

### Suffolk College
Rope Walk, Ipswich, Suffolk IP4 1LT
Telephone: 01473 255885
Business and Finance (HND), with specializations in Accounting, Business Systems and Technology, Financial Services, European Business, International Shipping and Trade, Marketing, Personnel or Tourism.

### University of Sunderland
Langham Tower, Ryhope Road, Sunderland SR2 7EE
Telephone: 0191 515 2423
Accounting (BA/BA Hons) with Business, Computing or Mathematics; Business and Finance (HND).

### University of Wales, Swansea
Singleton Park, Swansea, West Glamorgan SA2 8PP
Telephone: 01792 205678
Actuarial Studies (BSc Hons), available as a three-year course or four-year course with a year abroad.

### Swansea Institute of Higher Education
Townhill Campus, Townhill Road, Swansea, West Glamorgan SA2 0UT
Telephone: 01792 203482

Accounting (BA Hons); Business and Finance (HND).

### University of Teesside
Middlesbrough, Cleveland TS1 3BA
Telephone: 01642 218121
Accounting and Finance (BA/BSc Hons); Accounting with Law (BA/BSc Hons); Business and Finance (HND).

### Thames Valley University
St Mary's Road, Ealing, London W5 5RF
Telephone: 0181 231 2902
Accounting and Finance (BA/BA Hons); Accounting Studies Europe (BA/BA Hons), with choice of French, German or Spanish; Accounting and Law (BA/BA Hons); Accounting and Management Systems (BA/BA Hons); Business and Finance (HND), with Business Studies or Travel and Tourism options.

### The University of Ulster
Coleraine, County Londonderry BT52 1SA
Telephone: 01265 44141
Accounting (BA Hons); Banking and Finance (BA Hons); Accounting (Diploma), two-year course.

### The University of Warwick
Coventry CV4 7AL
Telephone: 01203 523523
Accounting and Financial Analysis (BSc Hons).

### West Herts College, Watford
Hempstead Road, Watford, Hertfordshire WD1 3EZ
Telephone: 01923 257565
Business Studies (HND) with Accounting and Financial Management option.

**West London Institute**
Gordon House, 300 St Margarets Road,
Twickenham, Middlesex TW1 1PT
Telephone: 0181 891 0121
Business and Finance (HND).

**University of Westminster**
309 Regent Street, London W1R 8AL
Telephone: 0171 911 5000
Business and Finance (HND).

**University of Wolverhampton**
Wulfruna Street, Wolverhampton
WV1 1SB
Telephone: 01902 321000
Accounting (BA/BA Hons);
Accounting and Finance (BA/BA
Hons); Financial Services (BA/BA
Hons); Business and Finance–Public
Administration (HND).

# Chapter 7 / **Further Information**

## Useful Addresses

### Accountancy

**Association of Accounting Technicians**
154 Clerkenwell Road, London
ECIR 3DA
Telephone: 0171 837 8600
Produces a guide to its education and training scheme, and a list of approved training assessment centres.

**Association of Corporate Treasurers**
12 Devereux Court, London WC2R 3JJ
Telephone: 0171 936 2354
Can supply brochure on professional education for corporate treasury.

**Chartered Association of Certified Accountants (ACCA)**
29 Lincoln's Inn Fields, London
WC2A 3EE
Telephone: 0171 242 6855

**Chartered Association of Certified Accountants (ACCA)**
Scottish Branch
2 Woodside Place, Glasgow G3 7QF
Telephone: 0141 309 4099

**Chartered Institute of Management Accountants**
63 Portland Place, London WIN 4AB

Telephone: 0171 637 2311
Produces a free guide to management accounting and the CIMA qualification.

**Chartered Institute of Public Finance and Accountancy**
3 Robert Street, London WC2N 6BH
Telephone: 0171 895 8823
Can supply a number of brochures on its syllabus and regulations and on careers in public-service accounting.

**Chartered Institute of Taxation**
12 Upper Belgrave Street, London
SWIX 8BB
Telephone: 0171 235 9381
The Institute of Taxation produces a list of firms employing tax trainees and an information pack on qualifications and careers in tax.

**Institute of Chartered Accountants in England and Wales**
Chartered Accountants Hall,
Moorgate Place, London EC2P 2BJ
Telephone: 0171 628 7060
Every autumn the ICAEW produces a training vacancies guide and a list of approved courses for accountancy education. It also has a brochure on

training outside public practice. All are available free on request from its student recruitment section, telephone: 0171 920 8677.

### Institute of Chartered Accountants in Ireland

Chartered Accountants House, 87–89 Pembroke Road, Ballsbridge, Dublin 4
Telephone: 003531 6680400
or
11 Donegal Square South, Belfast BT1 5JE
Telephone: 01232 321600

### Institute of Chartered Accountants of Scotland

27 Queen Street, Edinburgh, EH2 1LA
Telephone: 0131 225 5673

### Society of Practitioners of Insolvency

18–19 Long Lane, London EC1A 9HE
Telephone: 0171 600 3375
Produces the booklet *Making a Career as an Insolvency Practitioner*.

### Women in Accountancy

Each of the following professional bodies has a Women in Accountancy (WIA) representative: ACCA, ICAEW, CIMA, ICAS, CIPFA and ICAI (see above addresses for contact information). Aside from offering valuable networking opportunities, WIA can advise on training, career development, career breaks, retraining and part-time working.

## Banking

### Association of British Factors and Discounters

Information Office, 1 Northumberland Avenue, Trafalgar Square, London WC2N 5BW
Telephone: 0171 930 9112
Can send out annual review listing its members (most of which are subsidiaries of banks) and the services they offer.

### Banking Information Service

10 Lombard Street, London EC3V 9EL
Telephone: 0171 398 0066
Can supply brochures *Working in Banking* and *Action Plan for Applying for a Job* and information on salaries and university-sponsorship schemes.

### Building Societies Association

3 Savile Row, London W1X 1AF
Telephone: 0171 437 0655
Can supply leaflet *Going for it – Career Opportunities in Building Societies*.

### CFL Vision

PO Box 35, Wetherby, Yorkshire LS23 7EX
Telephone: 01937 541010
Can send out the video *Fact File on Building Societies* on free loan.

### Chartered Institute of Bankers

Emmanuel House, 4–9 Burgate Lane, Canterbury CT1 2XJ
Telephone: 01227 762600
Will send information on banking qualifications, syllabuses and regulations.

_90 St Shipsgate_
_Liverpool 87._

**Chartered Institute of Bankers –
Library and Information Service**
10 Lombard Street, London EC3V 9AS
Telephone: 0171 623 3531, extension
226  _0171 444 7111_
_there
uncinder_ The library is open free to members of
the Institute but there is a daily charge
for non-members. It has 20,000 books
plus information files, directories,
access to electronic databases, course
information and computer-based
learning programmes.

**Chartered Institute of Bankers in
Scotland**
19 Rutland Square, Edinburgh
EH1 2DE

Telephone: 0131 229 9869
Able to provide career and
qualifications information.

**Northern Ireland Bankers'
Association**
Stokes House, 17–25 College Square
East, Belfast BT1 6DE
Telephone: 01232 327551
Can give contact details for banks in
Northern Ireland.

**Women in Banking and Finance**
c/o Ann Leverrett, 55 Bourne Vale,
Bromley, Kent BR2 7NW
Telephone: 0181 462 3276

## Insurance and Personal Finance

**Actuarial Education Service**
Based at the Institute of Actuaries and
the Faculty of Actuaries (as listed).
Can supply information on courses
and exams.

**Association of British Insurers**
51–55 Gresham Street, London
EC2V 7HQ
Telephone: 0171 600 3333

**Association of Investment Trust
Companies**
Durrant House, 8–13 Chiswell Street,
London EC1Y 4YY
Telephone: 0171 588 5347
Produces a guide to investment trust
companies and an introduction to
investment trusts.

**British Insurance and Investment
Brokers' Association (BIIBA)**
BIIBA House, 14 Bevis Marks,
London EC3A 7NT
Telephone: 0171 623 9043
Can supply contact information on
national and international insurance
brokers.

**Chartered Insurance Institute**
Careers Information Officer, 20
Aldermanbury, London EC2V 7HY
Telephone: 0171 417 0495
CII has produced _The Business of Life_, a
careers brochure on financial services
which looks at six alternative career
paths: fund manager, actuary, life
underwriter, direct and independent
financial advisers and general
management. CII is also able to
supply brochures explaining its various
qualifications.

**Chartered Institute of Loss Adjusters**
376 Strand, London WC2R 0LR
Telephone: 0171 240 1496

**Faculty of Actuaries**
40–44 Thistle Street, Edinburgh
EH2 1EN
Telephone: 0131 220 4555

**IFA Promotion**
4th Floor, 28 Greville Street, London
EC1N 8SU
Telephone: 0171 831 4027
An organization promoting independent financial advice. It can supply a number of information packs including *Going it Alone*, designed for students preparing for higher education, *In For a Penny*, a student's guide to financial survival, and *Workwise*, a pack for those preparing to leave school or college.

**Institute of Actuaries**
Napier House, 4 Worcester Street, Oxford OX2 1AW
Telephone: 01865 794144
Can supply brochure *Becoming an Actuary*. A videotape called *Actuaries*, made jointly with the Faculty of Actuaries, is available from careers libraries.

**Insurance Brokers' Registration Council**
15 St Helen's Place, London EC3A 6DS
Telephone: 0171 588 4387

**Lloyd's of London**
1 Lime Street, London EC3M 7HA
Telephone: 0171 623 7100

**The Personal Investment Authority**
Hertsmere House, Hertsmere Road, London E14 4AB
Telephone: 0171 538 8860

## The City

**The Baltic Exchange**
St Mary Axe, London EC3A 8BH
Telephone: 0171 623 5501
The Baltic Exchange keeps a file containing the particulars of anyone looking for a job with its member firms. It can also supply a list of members.

**British Venture Capital Association**
Essex House, 12–13 Essex Street, London WC2R 3AA
Telephone: 0171 240 3846
Produces a guide to venture capital and a directory of its members.

**City Women's Network**
c/o Jeannette Masarati, PO Box 353, Uxbridge UB10 0UN
Telephone: 01895 272178

**City Business Library**
1 Brewer's Hall Garden (off London Wall), London EC2V 5BX
Telephone: 0171 638 8215

## Corporation of London

Guildhall, London EC2P 2EJ
Telephone: 0171 606 3030
The Corporation is the local authority for the City of London. Its public-relations office can supply information on the City's activities as an international financial centre.

## The Futures and Options Association

Roman Wall House, 1–2 Crutched Friars, London EC3N 2AN
Telephone: 0171 488 4610
Produces the booklet *An Option for your Future – A Career in the Derivatives Industry*.

## Institute of Chartered Shipbrokers

3 Gracechurch Street, London EC3V 0AT
Telephone: 0171 283 1361
Has booklets on TutorShip – its correspondence courses on the shipping business – its professional examinations, and a career in shipping.

## Institute of Investment Management and Research (IIMR)

211–213 High Street, Bromley, Kent BR1 1NY
Telephone: 0181 464 0811
Can supply general information and examination syllabus for the Investment Management Certificate.

## International Petroleum Exchange of London

International House, 1 St Katharine's Way, London E1 9UN
Telephone: 0171 481 0643
Has fact sheets on the types of contract traded, and on training and education.

## International Securities Market Association

7 Limeharbour, Docklands, London E14 9NQ
Telephone: 0171 538 5656

## Investor Relations Society

2nd Floor, 1 Bedford Street, London WC2E 9HD
Telephone: 0171 379 1763
Runs seminars on IR and can send out a brief introduction to the objectives and services of the society.

## London Bullion Market Association

6 Frederick's Place, London EC2R 8BT
Telephone: 0171 796 3067
Publishes a booklet on London's gold and silver trading market.

## London Clearing House

Roman Wall House, 1–2 Crutched Friars, London EC3N 2AN
Telephone: 0171 488 3200

## London Commodity Exchange

1 Commodity Quay, St Katharine Docks, London E1 9AX
Telephone: 0171 481 2080
Has a fact sheet on its contracts and operations.

## London Discount Market Association

39 Cornhill, London EC3V 3NU
Telephone: 0171 623 1020
Can give contact information on its members.

## London International Financial Futures and Options Exchange (LIFFE)

Cannon Bridge, London EC4R 3XX
Telephone: 0171 623 0444
Can supply an introductory brochure.

**London Metal Exchange**
E Section, 4th Floor, Plantation House,
31–35 Fenchurch Street, London
EC3M 3AP
Telephone: 0171 626 3311
Publishes a brochure on its history and
activities.

**London Stock Exchange**
London EC2N 1HP
Telephone: 0171 797 1000
Publishes a fact book on the Exchange
and its markets, and booklets, *A
Glossary of Stock Market Terms* and
*Introduction to the London Stock Exchange.*

**OMLX (The London Securities
and Derivatives Exchange)**
107 Cannon Street, London EC4N 5AD
Telephone: 0171 283 0678

**The Pensions Management
Institute**
PMI House, 4–10 Artillery Lane,
London E1 7LS
Telephone: 0171 247 1452
Can supply information on careers in
pensions management and on its
trustee-certificate qualification.

**Securities and Futures Authority**
Cottons Centre, Cottons Lane,
London SE1 2QB
Telephone: 0171 378 9000

**Securities and Investments Board**
Gavrelle House, 2–14 Bunhill Row,
London EC1Y 8RA
Telephone: 0171 638 1240
The SIB is the City's top investment
watchdog. It has a central register
with information on 50,000
investment firms. Information can be
accessed by calling the SIB or
through the New Prestel system,
which is available at larger libraries
and Citizens Advice Bureaux. The
register holds the name or trading
name of a firm and the address and
telephone number of its main place
of business. A free booklet on the
central register is available.

**Securities Institute**
Centurion House, 24 Monument
Street, London EC3R 8AJ
Telephone: 0171 626 3191
Can supply an information pack
and background on qualifications,
courses, seminars and educational
publications.

## Miscellaneous

**Law Society**
113 Chancery Lane, London
WC2A 1PL
Telephone: 0171 242 1222
Publishes booklets called *The Law
Degree Route to Qualification as a Solicitor*
and *The Non-Law Degree Route to Qualifi-
cation as a Solicitor.*

**Law Society of Northern Ireland**
Law Society House, 98 Victoria Street,
Belfast BT1 3JZ
Telephone: 01232 231614

**Law Society of Scotland**
The Law Society's Hall, 26
Drumsheugh Gardens, Edinburgh
EH3 7YR
Telephone: 0131 226 7411

# Chapter 8 / **Guide to the Jargon**

## Accountancy

**administration**   An alternative to liquidating an insolvent business. Administrators are appointed to run the business, selling bits of it when prudent to pay creditors. Once the debts have been paid the business may emerge from administration.

**administrative receivership**   Companies are put into receivership to recover debts on which they have defaulted. The official receivers sell assets – or the business itself as a going concern – to recover as much of the outstanding debt as possible. Receivership is more severe than administration. Companies that go into receivership are generally wound up.

**balance sheet**   A snapshot of a company or organization's financial status at a particular time, often its year-end, showing its assets and liabilities.

**bankruptcy**   Widely used as another word for insolvency, it refers specifically to individuals, rather than companies, who are unable to meet their liabilities.

**consolidated balance sheet**   A balance sheet that treats a number of linked companies (e.g. a parent company and its subsidiaries) as a single entity.

**creditor**   A bank or other lender to which an organization owes money.

**fixed assets**   Tangible assets such as land, property, manufacturing equipment, vehicles, etc.

**goodwill**   Intangible assets such as brands or trademarks, which are valuable to a company but are not as easy to quantify as fixed assets.

**gross**   Before tax is deducted.

**insolvency**   A company/organization becomes insolvent when it is unable to meet its debts due or when its assets are deemed insufficient to meet its liabilities.

**interim results**   A company's financial results for the first half of a year. These are released by companies quoted on the stock market (public limited companies) to give investors an indication of their performance. Interims, unlike figures for the full year, are not audited.

**limited liability**   A company with Ltd or plc after its name is a limited liability company. The owners of such companies cannot be called on personally to pay the company's debts if it becomes insolvent. They will lose only the money they have put into the company. This differs from the partners in a partnership and people operating as sole traders, who are liable for all debt incurred by their business.

**liquidation**   Winding up the affairs of an insolvent company and selling off its assets.

**net asset value**   The value of a company after all its debts have been paid.

**profit and loss account**   A statement showing the financial performance of a company or organization over a given period such as a year. The P&L account charts the revenue and expenditure, and profit or loss, made during that period.

**voluntary arrangement**   Liquidation, etc., carried out on the initiative of an organization or person rather than its creditors.

## Banking

**CHAPS**   The Clearing House Automated Payments System, used by the banks to settle cheques drawn from an account at one bank that are presented for payment into an account in another bank.

**charge card**   A credit payment card similar in nature to credit cards but with one important difference: the whole balance must be paid back every month. American Express and Diners Club are two of the best known charge cards.

**clearing bank**    A bank that has many cheques to clear each day and is an active lender/borrower on the money markets. The big four high-street banks and other large retail banks are clearers.

**credit card**    Payment cards issued by banks that enable you to make purchases on credit. The issuing company makes money by charging interest on any outstanding balance that is not repaid by the due date each month. Visa and Mastercard/Access are the big names that run credit card systems for the banks.

**debit card**    Payment cards issued by banks that deduct money direct from your bank account in the same way as a cheque. Well-known debit card systems are Switch and Delta.

**factoring**    Factors collect debts on behalf of clients and advance them a proportion of those debts to help their cash-flow. Factors may also take over payment chasing and processing responsibilities on behalf of their clients. Most of the leading factoring operations are owned by banks.

**invoice discounting**    A simple funding service offered by factors to their clients which does not include the full administrative support of factoring.

**machine room**    The part of a bank that handles processing tasks such as dealing with cheques.

**rescheduling**    Rearranging the terms of a loan. It usually means giving borrowers with financial difficulties longer to pay back the capital and interest.


## Insurance and Personal Finance

**broker**    Intermediary registered with the Insurance Brokers Registration Council.

**composite insurer**    One that offers insurance in a wide variety of areas.

**endowment policy**    A fixed-term life assurance policy, where the insurer pays out on the death of the insured during the term, or at the end of the term if the insured has survived. An endowment mortgage offers an alternative to a repayment mortgage.

Instead of paying back the capital and interest, the buyer pays premiums to the life assurance company which, when the policy matures, should be sufficient to repay the loan.

**IFA**  Independent Financial Adviser.

**Lloyd's Name**  An underwriting member of Lloyd's of London. Names agree personally to cover the risks underwritten on the market.

**managing agent**  A person permitted by Lloyd's to organize the business of a syndicate.

**Personal Equity Plan (PEP)**  A way of investing in shares that has tax advantages. PEPs enable individuals to avoid paying capital gains tax on profits and income tax on dividends.

**premium**  The amount of money paid to an insurance company in return for insurance cover.

**reinsurance**  The cover purchased by insurance companies from other insurers to protect them from large losses.

**repayment mortgage**  A mortgage where the capital and interest is repaid over a fixed period, often twenty-five years.

**syndicates**  The groups formed by Lloyd's Names to spread their risk.

**unit trust**  A portfolio of holdings in various securities divided into units and managed by a professional investment organization.

## The City

**arbitrage**  Buying securities, currencies or commodities only to sell them almost immediately afterwards on a different market. The object is to make a profit by exploiting the differences between the buying and selling prices on different markets.

**arbitrageur**  Someone engaged in arbitrage.

**basis points**  Used to measure changes in interest rates, a basis point is a hundredth of a per cent.

**bear**  Someone who sells a security in the hope of buying it back later at a lower price.

**bear market**  A falling market.

**BIFFEX**   A freight futures market used to hedge against movements in freight price.

**bill of exchange**   A bill made out by one party and addressed to another requiring the addressee to pay a fixed amount of money by a certain date. These are traded on the money market.

**bond**   A type of security issued by governments, banks, corporations, etc., as a way of raising money. In effect, a bond is an IOU bought by investors. The issuer of the bond pays the investors a fixed rate of interest during the period of the loan.

**bull**   Someone who buys a security in the hope that it will go up in price.

**bull market**   A rising market.

**call option**   The right, but *not* the obligation, to buy shares at an agreed price on a future date (see Options contract).

**certificate of deposit (CD)**   A certificate given by a bank to a depositor that can be traded on the money market. The depositor is able to get high levels of interest by putting their money in the bank for a fixed term but can sell the CD to someone else if they want to get their lump sum back at short notice.

**clearing**   The process of matching, guaranteeing and registering transactions.

**clearing house**   An institution that undertakes clearing.

**closed-end fund**   An investment company with a fixed amount of capital whose shares are traded on the Stock Exchange. Investment trusts are closed-end funds.

**commercial paper (CP)**   A way of borrowing on the money market. Investors buy CPs that have been issued by companies that want to raise money.

**commission**   The fee that brokers charge their clients for dealing on their behalf.

**commodities exchange**   An investment exchange dealing in commodities such as oil, metal and foodstuffs.

**convertible bond**   A bond that can be converted into shares in a company.

**coupon**   The interest rate on a bond or other financial instrument.

**CREST**   An electronic settlement system.

**delivery**   The settlement of a futures contract.

**derivatives**   The generic term for futures and options.

**dividend**   Money paid to shareholders out of a company's profits.

**equity**   Another word for share. It is a company's capital as owned by its shareholders.

**Eurobond**   A bond issued in one country that is denominated in the currency of another country.

**expiry**   The date on which the right to an option expires. Once an option has expired it ceases to exist.

**flotation**   When a company switches from being privately owned to publicly owned and its shares are offered on the stock market for the first time.

**foreign exchange**   The foreign exchange market, often shortened to forex, is the buying and selling of international currencies by investors and speculators.

**FT-SE 100 Share Index**   Commonly known as the Footsie, this is an index of the 100 leading UK shares on the London Stock Exchange. It is produced in association with the *Financial Times*.

**futures contract**   A legally binding contract traded on a futures exchange such as LIFFE for a specified quantity of a commodity or financial instrument. The parties involved agree to buy or sell a specified asset at a fixed point in the future for a price set at the time of the trade.

**gearing**   A company's debts in relation to its equity capital, usually expressed as a percentage.

**gilts**   Short for Gilt-Edged Securities. These are loans taken out by the Government to help fund its spending. Gilts are also called government bonds.

**hedging**   Buying or selling to offset any adverse changes in asset prices.

**insider dealing**   A criminal offence whereby someone who has 'price-sensitive' information about a company that is not known generally to the market trades in that company's shares to make a profit.

**investment trust**   A company listed on the Stock Exchange whose primary business is to invest in the shares of other companies. They are closed-end funds (*q.v.*).

**issue**   The first time a security is sold.

**junk bonds**   High risk, high yielding bonds.

**last trading day**   The last day on which trading is allowed in a futures contract with a given delivery or settlement month.

**leveraged buy-out**   Using debt in the form of junk bonds or bank loans to take over a company.

**listed company**   A company whose shares appear on the Stock Exchange's daily Official List.

**margin**   The amount of money that must be deposited to provide protection for both parties in a derivatives trade.

**market capitalization**   The total value of all the shares in a public company at a given time. It is worked out by multiplying the number of shares issued by their current market price. Often called capitalization.

**market maker**   A broker/dealer member of the Stock Exchange, which is obliged to buy and sell the specific securities for which it is registered. By quoting a buying and selling price the firm *makes* the market for a particular security.

**multiple**   See Price/earnings ratio.

**offer**   The price at which a market maker sells securities to an investor.

**options contract**   Similar to a futures contract in that traders buy or sell financial instruments based on a view of these assets' likely future performance. The big difference is that the buyer of an options contract is purchasing the right, but *not* the obligation, to buy or sell a futures contract on a particular date. The seller of an option is, however, obliged to buy or sell if the buyer decides to exercise their option.

**premium**   (1) The price of an option (in derivatives trading) determined by traders on the Exchange floor. (2) The difference between the issue price and market price of a new security if it rises in value immediately after it is issued.

**price/earnings ratio**  A company's current share price divided by its most recent earnings per share. It is a guide to market confidence in a company – the higher the p/e ratio the more confident investors are. The p/e ratio is sometimes referred to as the multiple.

**principal**  An investor who buys or sells on their own account at their own risk, as opposed to a broker who acts on behalf of somebody else.

**private placement/placing**  Where a company sells shares directly to specific investors.

**put option**  An option that gives the buyer the right, but *not* the obligation, to sell futures or shares at the exercise price on or before the date on which the contract expires (see Options contract).

**rights issue**  Selling new shares to existing shareholders to raise capital.

**securities**  Collective term for stocks and shares.

**settlement**  Transferring shares and money between buyers and sellers.

**shares**  The capital of a company split into parts of an equal size. Shares in the UK's major public companies are bought and sold by investors on the London Stock Exchange and consequently may rise or fall in price.

**shareholder**  A person or organization owning shares in a company.

**spot price**  The current value of an asset.

**spread**  The difference between a market maker's buying and selling price.

**stag**  Someone who applies for shares in a company at the time of an issue in the hope of selling them on at a profit as soon as trading in those shares begins.

**Stock Exchange Alternative Trading Service (SEATS)**  A computer-based price-information system introduced by the London Stock Exchange in 1993 for 'less liquid' securities. It complements SEAQ (*q.v.*).

**Stock Exchange Automated Quotations (SEAQ)**  The

London Stock Exchange's computer-based price information system.

**stocks**   (1) Another word for bonds; fixed-interest securities denominated in money terms. (2) Sometimes (confusingly!) used to mean the same as shares.

**swaps**   (1) The exchange of securities of the same value. (2) A type of foreign exchange derivatives deal.

**Third Market**   The market introduced in January 1987 for securities too untested for the Unlisted Securities Market.

**underlying instrument**   The conventional stock or share on which a derivative is based.

**underwriting**   A guarantee to buy or find buyers for some or all of an issue of stocks or shares. This is generally carried out by banks in return for a fee.

**Unlisted Securities Market (USM)**   The London Stock Exchange's market for medium-size companies that do not qualify for, or do not wish to have, a full listing. It is frequently used as a stepping stone to the main market.

**white knight**   A company that rescues another company which is in financial trouble. Sometimes white knights save other companies from hostile takeover bids.


## Miscellaneous

**asset**   An investment or part of a business that is of value and may generate earnings.

**SRO**   A Self-Regulatory Organization responsible for regulating the conduct of investment firms. SROs include the Securities and Futures Authority (SFA) and the Personal Investment Authority (PIA).

**yield**   The return on an investment, normally expressed as a percentage.

# Chapter 9 / **Getting a Job**

## How to Handle the Job Hunt

Tips on getting ahead have been included in the earlier chapters, but all are academic if you don't approach the job hunt in the right way. Finding a job is always hard work – especially financial jobs, which are highly coveted. You need vast reserves of resilience, persistence and determination. Vacancies often attract hundreds of applicants so it could take some time – and a few rejections – before you finally strike it lucky.

### First Steps

It is important to have a clear idea of which aspect of finance will best suit you, so research the subject to find out what job areas appeal. The best way to find out what a particular job is like is to talk to people who do it. Call people in your target area and ask if they would be prepared to chat to you for a quarter of an hour about their work. The worst they can do is say no, but you may be pleasantly surprised by the number of people who will be happy to do so.

Choose the time of your call carefully and take into account the person's job: a City dealer, for example, probably won't have time to spare while the market in which they work is open for business so get in touch at the end of the day, after the market has closed. Make it clear that you are just looking for information and are not expecting to be offered a job. As well as asking what their work involves, you could sound them out about the state of the industry, trends in the way things are going or what employers look for.

Don't abuse their generosity: if you asked for fifteen minutes of their time, try not to take up more unless they are obviously happy to carry on – and remember to send a thank-you letter soon after.

If your research reveals obvious gaps in your training or knowledge, do something about it, whether it's enrolling on a word-processing course or attending an industry conference. As well as improving your skills base, you will also be providing an employer with a positive demonstration of your commitment and enthusiasm.

Make sure you *know* about the industry. Read the specialist press and the business pages of the newspapers so that you're up to date on the issues affecting it. That way, you will also know when companies are expanding or have won new business and might, therefore, be looking to recruit more staff.

If you are a student planning to break into finance after you leave university, you need to start gathering skills, practical experience and training as soon as possible to give you the edge over all the other thousands of graduates who will be chasing jobs and postgraduate courses in the same field. Make the most of any free training on offer in your university or college, in computing or languages, for example. Relevant work experience counts for a lot, and as much of it as possible, so good vacation jobs are vital. If you have secretarial skills, you may be able to find temping work. The other way of getting that all-important experience (and real insider view) is by offering to work for free. A good work placement will teach you more about the job than any careers book or counsellor can and the experience gained can be more valuable than all the paper qualifications in the world when it comes to getting a permanent job. It is also a chance to make useful contacts and, if it goes well, will stand you in good stead when vacancies come up.

## Making the Most of Work Experience

• Lots of students look for work experience in the holidays, so you're more likely to find something if you can work during term-time. Apply at least a couple of months in advance of when you want to work, as it can be difficult to find a place.

• Be reliable. Even though you are not being paid a fortune – if paid at all – you should behave professionally, arriving on time and not leaving before the end of the working day.

• Most of the work you are given will be thoroughly mundane (would *you* trust an inexperienced student with anything else?) but if you do the photocopying and tea-making with good grace you will make a good impression. Work with enthusiasm, and offer to help before being asked, and you will definitely be remembered. However boring the tasks, do them *all* well: every little detail matters.

• It is always better to ask questions if you are doing something you don't understand than to blunder ahead and get it wrong. Whenever you ask a question, pay attention to the answer and write everything down so that you don't irritate people by asking the same things over and over again.

• Remember people's names: draw a plan of the office with names by desks to jog your memory.

• Try to move around departments to get a flavour of each, rather than staying in one place the whole time.

• How you handle people on the phone will be noticed, so be polite, try to sound authoritative, and make sure when you take messages that you get the person's name and number and note down the date and time. Watch how other people deal with callers for hints on how to behave. Don't take the opportunity of the 'free' phones to call all your friends: if you must make a personal call, ask permission first.

• Use your initiative. If someone looks really busy, offer to help; if the phone rings at an empty desk, answer it. Ask if there is any

outstanding filing you could do or if the bookshelves need tidying. If there is really nothing, use the time to practise on the computer.
• If the placement was successful, ask someone you worked with closely if they would provide a reference for you. Try to get them to do it before you leave or very soon after, before they forget who you are. If there is anyone you get on particularly well with, let them know you would love to hear when any jobs are going and stay in contact.

## Finding a Job

Look for jobs in the following daily newspapers:
*Financial Times* (Wednesday, banking and finance; Thursday, accountancy)
*Independent* (Wednesday)
*The Times* (Thursday)
*Daily Telegraph* (Thursday)
*Daily Mail* (Thursday)
*Guardian* (Thursday/Saturday)
*Evening Standard* (Daily)

In the following Sunday newspapers:
*Sunday Times*
*Observer*
*Sunday Telegraph*
*Independent on Sunday*
*Mail on Sunday*

In the following trade publications:
*Accountancy Age*: published weekly by VNU Business Publications, it carries a wide range of accountancy jobs. Annual subscription rate £100. Telephone: 0171 316 9000.
*Financial Adviser*: published weekly by Financial Times Magazines, it carries recruitment advertising for IFAs. It is a controlled-circulation title – that is, it is not generally available on subscription – but may be taken by the better reference libraries. Call 0171 896 2525 for more information.

*Money Marketing*: the weekly newspaper for the personal investment intermediary carrying jobs for IFAs. Published by Centaur Communications, price £1.50. Telephone: 0171 287 5678.

*Post Magazine*: The biggest selling UK insurance journal carrying a broad cross-section of insurance jobs. Published weekly by Timothy Benn Publishing, price £2. Subscriptions 0181 289 7954.

And in the weekly newsstand magazines *Investors' Chronicle* and *The Economist*.

When you see a job advertisement that interests you, study it carefully. What sort of qualities and experience do you think the employer is looking for? How can you demonstrate that you have them? Don't be afraid to apply for a job just because you don't have every single quality asked for – employers know that the perfect candidate is a rare creature. As long as you meet *most* of the requirements, you're in with a chance.

However, sitting back and waiting for the perfect advertisement to appear in the paper could take years – so don't. Go out looking instead. It has been estimated that only 10 per cent of people find jobs by answering newspaper ads and many employers try to cut costs and avoid a deluge of applications by relying on word of mouth to find suitable candidates. Write directly to the person in charge of the department or programme, rather than to Personnel, and specify the kind of work for which you are looking. Your letter may then be passed on to Personnel but not before it has been seen by the person who makes the decisions about whom to employ.

Networking is one of the best ways of finding a job, so increase your visibility and experience by attending relevant courses or industry conferences and talks. If anyone you know is employed in a company for which you want to work, ask them to keep an ear to the ground and an eye on the in-house noticeboards and magazines to find out if any jobs are going. Some companies offer a cash incentive to employees who can introduce new staff to the company and save them advertising.

Get in touch with the specialist financial-recruitment consultancies. Although they are mostly asked to find experienced candidates for their clients they sometimes have more junior vacancies on their books. Even if they don't they can be a useful source of information about which companies may be looking to recruit in the near future and the kind of vacancies they are likely to have. Once again, be courteous and succinct: recruitment consultants are often happy to spare a few minutes to give some free advice, but most are extremely busy and won't appreciate you wasting their time.

## Recruitment Consultancies

### Accountancy

**Barclay Simpson**
Hamilton House, 1 Temple Avenue, Victoria Embankment, London
EC4Y 0HA
Telephone: 0171 936 2601

**Hays Accountancy Personnel**
14 Great Castle Street, Oxford Circus, London WIN 7AD
Telephone: 0171 436 5511

**Chartac Recruitment Services**
The Institute of Chartered Accountants in England and Wales, PO Box 433, Chartered Accountants' Hall, Moorgate Place, London
EC2P 2BJ
Telephone: 0171 920 8681
Chartac, the ICAEW's free career advice and recruitment service, can help with arranging interviews, making contacts and preparing CVs

**Reed Accountancy**
Tolworth Tower, Tolworth, Surrey
KT6 7EL
Telephone: 0181 399 5221
Has a network of 60 offices across the UK. Also advertises jobs on the

Internet at http//www.reed.co.uk./reed/ from where it is also possible to download an application form.

### Insurance and Personal Financial Advisers

**Acme Appointments**
Guild House, 36–38 Fenchurch Street, London EC3M 3DQ
Telephone: 0171 929 5252

**Adjusting Appointments**
6 York Place, Leeds LS1 2DS
Telephone: 0113 2460525

**Centrepoint**
Alma House, Alma Road, Reigate, Surrey RH2 0AX
Telephone: 01737 240107

**DSL Insurance Personnel**
100 George Lane, South Woodford, London E18 1AD
Telephone: 0181 518 8844

**Hillman Saunders**
78–79 Leadenhall Street, London
EC3A 3DH
Telephone: 0171 929 0707

**Independent Insurance Appointments**
6 York Place, Leeds LS1 2DS
Telephone: 0113 2440846
Also offices in Leicester, Manchester and Newcastle.

**Insurance Personnel**
88 Gracechurch Street, London EC3V 0DN
Telephone: 0171 283 8383
Also offices in Cambridge, Croydon, Maidstone, Manchester and Wakefield.

**Insurance Personnel Selection (IPS Group)**
Lloyd's Avenue House, 6 Lloyd's Avenue, London EC3N 3ES
Telephone: 0171 481 8111
or
Ludgate House, 28 Ludgate Hill, Birmingham B3 1DX
Telephone: 0121 605 8999

**Insurance Recruitment Group**
Guild House, 36–38 Fenchurch Street, London EC3M 3DQ
Telephone: 0171 929 5252

**Inter Selection**
16 Byward Street, London EC3R 5BA
Telephone: 0171 480 7220
Also has offices in Bristol, Birmingham, Manchester, Leeds, Glasgow and Edinburgh.

**Jonathan Wren & Co**
1 New Street, London EC2M 4TP
Telephone: 0171 623 1266
Also in Bristol, telephone: 0117 9225762

**Joslin Rowe**
Forum House, 15–18 Lime Street, London EC3M 7AP
Telephone: 0171 283 6008

**Kelly Insurance**
48A Station Road, Redhill, Surrey RH1 1PH
Telephone: 01737 768588

**Kingfisher Corporation**
PO Box 2000, Shoreham-by-Sea, BN43 5EH
Telephone: 01273 441144

**Nicholas Moore Selection**
150 Minories, London EC3N 1LS
Telephone: 0171 264 2132

**Recruitment Link Nationwide**
Stort House, 84 Stortford Hall Park, Bishop's Stortford, Herts CM23 5AN
Telephone: 01279 653617
Specializes in jobs for sales consultants and financial planning advisers.

**Reed Insurance**
24 Lime Street, London EC3
Telephone: 0171 621 0733
Also branches in Kingston, Reading, Maidstone, Southampton and Croydon.

**Vincent Knight Sanchez**
108 Kingston Road, Wimbledon, London SW19 1LX
Telephone: 0181 542 4515
Specialist in actuarial recruitment.

## The City

**Banking Personnel**
41–42 London Wall, London EC2M 5TB
Telephone: 0171 588 0781

**Citifocus**
12A Finsbury Square, London EC2A 1AS
Telephone: 0171 588 9552

**Joslin Rowe Associates**
Bell Court House, 11 Blomfield Street,
London EC2M 7AY
Telephone: 0171 638 5286

**Jonathan Wren Financial
Recruitment Consultants**
1 New Street, London EC2M 4TP
Telephone: 0171 623 1266

## Written Applications

The Perfect CV

The purpose of a CV is to get you an interview – and that applies whether you are writing to an employer on spec or applying for an advertised vacancy. The idea is to make it a tempting taster so that they will want to find out more. It is not meant to tell the whole story of your life and should never be more than two sides long – no employer is going to want to read more than that. For recent graduates, one page is enough. Tailor your CV to each different job for which you apply, emphasizing or downplaying different aspects as relevant. Remember to adapt your CV as the years go on, adding, cutting and rewriting. For example, the further away you get from your schooldays, the less relevant your GCSEs become, so prune back the details as more relevant experience supersedes them. Neither do you need to carry on putting down the holiday job you did when you were sixteen.

There are many different styles of CV and which you choose is a question of taste. The traditional and most widely recognized CV is one that follows a chronological format. After your basic personal details (name, address, telephone number; date of birth, nationality), give your career history, starting with your current or most recent job, and working backwards. State the job title, company name, period of employment, give a brief job description and mention any special achievements. Describe your current job in most detail; be more succinct about any before that. After Career History, list Educational Qualifications, again working backwards. You may also wish to include Other Information (e.g. driving licence, foreign languages, computer skills).

Alternatively, you could opt for a functional or skills CV. It is not as common but is useful if you have had frequent job changes, if you are trying to change career direction or if you have a limited career history but have acquired relevant skills and experience in other areas, such as voluntary work or work experience. It also takes the emphasis off any gaps. Under headings such as Financial Experience, Administrative Abilities or Communications Skills, summarize your experience in those areas. If you are applying for an advertised job, make sure you match your headings to the qualities asked for in the advertisement. Voluntary work is a particularly good source of transferable skills: teaching adult literacy or English as a second language calls for effective communication skills and an ability to motivate others.

A third option is a targeted CV, best used when you are applying for jobs on spec rather than in response to particular job advertisements. The emphasis is on aiming for a specific position and explaining why you are qualified for it. Under the heading 'Job Target' state the position for which you are aiming. Then, under headings such as 'Capabilities' and 'Achievements', list your skills and talents that relate to your prospective position and include what you have done so far that shows you would be able to perform in the job. Further headings should include 'Work Experience' and 'Education', as on a chronological CV.

Whichever format you choose, there are certain basic rules to follow:

- Use good quality white or off-white paper. Avoid anything fancy or gimmicky.
- Make the layout as attractive and accessible as possible: use a clear, easy-to-read typeface and leave wide margins and spaces between sections.
- Avoid long sentences. An employer wants to see the key facts at a glance and won't be impressed by rambling prose. Keep phrases short, punchy and active, starting with a verb – 'developed new cost control system', 'beat sales target'. You don't need to say 'I' every time – who else would you be talking about in your CV?

- Cut out anything inessential. You don't need to include addresses of employers or educational institutions. If you have a degree it is not necessary to itemize every GCSE subject and grade (although many employers of graduates also look for good A level results as an indicator of consistency).

- A CV should always be typed – and *well* typed. If you can't do it yourself or don't have access to a machine, get someone who can and does to do it for you.

- There is no need to include referees here, unless you have such stunningly good ones that it would impress an employer. Never give anyone's name as a referee without checking with them first.

- Check, double check and triple check your CV – then give it to a friend to check again. Any mistakes will count against you.

- Eliminate the negative. A CV is a selling document, not the place to advertise every exam you have ever failed or career setback you have faced.

- Don't include current salary details unless asked to do so. People will make certain assumptions about you and your worth if you give them specific figures, and you could put yourself out of the running by earning too little or too much. Plenty of time to talk money later.

- Include interests and hobbies if you have little work experience; otherwise, leave them off unless they demonstrate a skill or quality relevant to the job or are so unusual that they will intrigue the interviewer.

- If applying for jobs abroad, enclose a passport photograph of yourself – this is done more commonly in other European countries than it is here.

- If you are responding to a job advertisement, make sure that the skills you highlight in your CV match those specified in the ad.

- Extra skills such as computer literacy and foreign languages are valuable, but don't make them up to impress. If you claim to have fluent French, for example, you could find an interviewer asking you some questions in that language.

**Positive/active words that stand out on CVs**

achieved • administered • analysed • built • capable • competent
communicated • consistent • controlled • co-ordinated • created
designed • developed • directed • economical • effective
efficient • established • expanded • experienced • guided
implemented • improved • initiated • increased • introduced • led
managed • monitored • organized • participated • positive
processed • produced • professional • proficient • profitable
qualified • ran • repaired • researched • resourceful • responsible
skilled • sold • specialized • stable • successful • supervised
trained • versatile • volunteered • wrote

The Covering Letter

Never send off a CV or an application form without a covering
letter – you will be missing a great opportunity to sell yourself. (If
you have a glowing testimonial or letter of recommendation from
a former employer, you could enclose that too.) Keep it short and
to the point: it should fit onto one sheet, preferably on the same,
high-quality paper as your CV.

Put your address in the top right-hand corner or centred at the
top of the page, and the date and address of the person to whom
you are sending it below that on the left-hand side. Make sure you
address the letter to someone by name rather than 'the Personnel
Officer' or 'Dear Sir/Madam'. Telephone the company first to
find out, and always check the spelling. The correct ending to a
letter addressed to a person by name is 'Yours sincerely'; 'Yours
faithfully' is only used when the addressee is Dear Sir/Madam.

Make sure that the letter is tidy: if there are several applicants
for a job, it is easy to start by discarding those whose replies are
scruffy or ill-prepared. Typing looks smarter, unless the employer
specifically requests a hand-written letter, in which case draft it on

a rough piece of paper first so that you can write the final letter without mistakes. Use blue or, preferably, black ink; other colours are generally frowned upon and green is considered the trademark of a loony.

With any job application, it is important that your spelling, grammar and punctuation are correct. If you are applying for a specific job, say how you heard about it, and if there is a reference number, include it. If you are writing at the suggestion of someone known personally to the employer or someone who is well-known in the field, mention it straight away. Keep the language simple: many people make the mistake of using over-formal, flowery phrases which sound stilted and unnatural. State briefly why you are a strong candidate and emphasize what you have to offer the employer. It is not good enough to say 'I'd love to work in the City'. So would a million others. Draw attention to the relevant bits of your CV but don't go into details: save that for the interview.

Don't write a fabulous letter, then ruin the effect by cramming it into a tiny little envelope. Your paper should never be folded more than twice, so make sure your envelope is A4, A5 or 220 × 110 mm.

## Application Forms

Many companies, especially large organizations such as the big accountancy firms, banks and insurance companies, ask all job applicants to fill in an application form rather than sending in a CV. It makes it easier for them to find the information they need to know quickly, which is invaluable when dealing with large numbers of applicants.

Photocopy the blank form and do a rough version of your answers on the photocopy; when you are happy with it, copy them on to the original. Complete all sections, however irrelevant they might seem. Don't leave the Further Information box blank: this is your chance to shine and say things you haven't been able to say elsewhere. Look back at the advertisement to see what they were asking for and use this opportunity to prove how well you match the description. Write legibly and in black ink: the form will probably be photocopied and blue ink doesn't photocopy well.

Take a photocopy of the finished form as a useful reference for the next time you have to fill one in.

## Interviews

Interviews can be nerve-racking, especially for first-time job-hunters – and the more you want the job, the worse it is. Nerves come, in a large part, from feeling unready and unprepared, so the more you plan ahead, the better your chances and the better you will feel on the day. Research may be time-consuming but it is worth the effort: it shows initiative and motivation and will give you a great advantage over candidates who haven't bothered. If you are ignorant about the company's work, then you are obviously not very interested in them or, presumably, the job. Don't be careless: confusing the company's products, services or clients with those of a rival won't win you any friends.

You should already be reading the relevant trade press to keep up to date on the industry. If you are going for a front-office job in the City of London it is a real plus to be able to demonstrate that you have a genuine interest in the workings of finance and investment management. Some candidates do this by running their own hypothetical investment portfolios, usually of shares quoted on the London Stock Exchange (the prices are published in the *Financial Times*). To do this you don't have to buy any shares: just pick a selection of companies that you think are likely to do well and chart the progress of their shares over a period of a few months. Then bring a neatly presented record of this along to your interview. It won't matter if the shares you have chosen perform badly – even the experts often get it wrong. At least you will have shown a prospective employer that you have the interest and initiative to follow the financial markets. But be prepared to answer questions on why you picked the companies you did!

Whatever the job you are going for, the following tips apply:

• Expect to be asked about your personal life and leisure interests as well as strictly work issues. The employer is trying to put together a picture of you as a whole person.

• If you are already working, prepare a clear, succinct précis of your job and be prepared to answer questions on any aspect of it. Past performance is the main thing employers have to rely on when it comes to assessing how well you would do with them, so make sure you feed them relevant examples of past experience. How have you shown initiative, reliability, creativity, organizational flair? Can you work well under pressure or adapt to changing conditions? What computer systems can you use?

• Be ready to explain why you are interested in this job. Sounds obvious, yes, but it is surprising how many people don't think it through.

• Be prepared for tests. These vary, but for many financial jobs they will often be numerical in nature.

• Straightforward questions about your studies, qualifications or job history are relatively easy to answer and you should certainly expect to be asked any of the questions in the box below. Some interviewers like to spring horrors on you such as 'How would your best friend/worst enemy/colleagues describe you?' or 'What are your strengths/weaknesses?' You are unlikely to think of a suitable answer on the spot so it helps to think ahead and have examples prepared. *Great Answers to Tough Interview Questions*, Martin John Yate (Kogan Page £6.99), has some great ideas on how to answer questions which have the potential to catch you out.

• If you are going for your first job after school or university, you are unlikely to have much work experience so you will have to look to other areas for skills and experience to offer employers. Did you participate in team sports? Take leading roles in school plays? Serve on a hall of residence committee? Deliver seminars? Undertake extensive or unusual travel during vacations? Have you done voluntary work or any work placements during the holidays, served time on a local community committee or been involved in an advisory board? Be prepared to answer questions about why

**Questions you're likely to be asked**

Tell me about yourself

What makes you right for this job?

Why do you want to work for us?

What do you like/dislike in your current job?

Why do you want to leave your current job?

Where do you see yourself in five years' time?

Tell me all about your current job

What computer systems have you worked on?

How do you feel about working long hours?

---

you did these things and what you feel you have gained from them. Even things that seem irrelevant to you may help to give an employer a fuller picture of you.

• As much as anything, they want evidence that you are reliable and responsible so even non-finance-related work experience at weekends or in vacations could illustrate those qualities. If you have paid for any postgraduate studies yourself, it shows strong motivation and commitment so make sure you mention it.

• If you are a bit rusty at interviews try to run the whole thing through with a more practised friend beforehand, getting them to play the interviewer: they may come up with more possible questions you hadn't thought of. You may feel silly at first but it *will* help. Ask for honest feedback and don't get upset or defensive if there are negative points, as that will discourage further comment. Don't over-rehearse or you will end up sounding stilted and unnatural when you want to appear spontaneous and relaxed.

• You don't always get much notice of an interview so don't leave all your preparation until the letter arrives. Start thinking about it when you write your application.

• Don't spend so long worrying about the questions you will be asked that you forget the basics. Get plenty of sleep the night before the interview. Work out in advance how you are going to get there and how long it will take – and allow extra time for delays. Make sure a couple of days ahead that your clothes are clean and ready.

## On the Day

### Getting In the Mood

- Be positive! If you have been asked for an interview, they are obviously interested in you. To get to this stage you have probably already beaten hundreds of others and may be on a short-list of between six and twelve. The employer already believes you are *capable* of the job. All you have to do is prove it.
- Do anything to help boost your confidence: read a favourite poem or inspirational book on the way to the interview, listen to 'up' music on your Walkman, remind yourself of all the times you have triumphed against the odds or all the things you have done that make you feel proud.
- Reread your letter/CV/application form and be ready to answer questions on anything you have included. Take copies with you in case the interviewer has mislaid them.
- Take a spare pair of tights, needle and cotton (for emergency repairs), phonecard and small change (for parking or phone calls). Make sure you have the company's phone number so that you can call in an emergency, and don't forget to take their address.
- Set out in plenty of time and aim to arrive ten to fifteen minutes early. Don't expect buses or trains to turn up on time or assume that you will find a parking space easily. Use any waiting time to watch the people around you, read any internal noticeboards or in-house newsletters, and generally try to get a feel of the place.
- Don't smoke or drink shortly before the interview: smelling of smoke or alcohol isn't going to impress any interviewer.

## Looking the Part

Don't underestimate the importance of appearance. Research has shown that an interviewer's impression of you will be made up of 55 per cent on how you look, 38 per cent on how you sound and only 7 per cent on what you say. First impressions are quickly formed and hard to change, and although your interview might last an hour, a decision has probably been made within the first four or five minutes.

• Your clothes don't need to be expensive – nobody expects someone fresh out of college to waltz in wearing Armani – but they must be presentable and clean. Make sure they are comfortable, too: you can't concentrate on the interview if you are too busy worrying about wayward buttons or squirming around because your skirt is too tight.

• Dress appropriately for the organization. As a general rule think smart rather than trendy. Financial companies usually have a more conventional and unadventurous dress code than, say, media or hi-tech employers. Some experts recommend going to watch staff leaving or entering the workplace, so that you can get an idea of the corporate image and tailor your interview outfit accordingly (same kind of clothes but a bit smarter).

• Heels look smarter than flat – but not *too* high – and studies suggest that wearing light, natural make-up rather than none increases your chances of success by 20 per cent.

• Don't smoke, even if invited to do so – it looks messy. And unless you're ultra-relaxed refuse tea or coffee – they provide more scope for disaster.

• Don't go into the interview room clutching carrier bags of shopping or a dripping wet coat and umbrella: leave any encumbrances with the receptionist.

• Try to appear confident, even if you are quaking inside. Walk in confidently and sit upright but relaxed in the chair. Leaning slightly forward shows attention and interest. Look the interviewer in the eye but don't fix them with an unwavering stare.

• Speak up and, if you tend to gabble when nervous, make a conscious effort to speak more slowly. Try to sound enthusiastic. Keep your arms and legs uncrossed, don't shift around in your seat and try not to fiddle with jewellery or your hair. Merely sitting comfortably gives the desired impression of calm and confidence.

• However nervous you feel, *smile*! Most interviewers base their final decisions on gut feeling, and it is only natural that they will warm more to someone who appears relaxed and friendly, whom they think will be pleasant to work with as well as able to do the job.

• Don't save your best behaviour for the interviewer alone: be just as pleasant to the receptionist and anyone else with whom you make contact – they may be asked for their impressions.

## In the Interview

• If the interviewer starts by asking you a few general questions, such as how your journey to the interview was, they are only trying to put you at your ease so don't go into great detail.

• A bit of humour or wit at appropriate moments will make you more memorable to an interviewer and provide light relief in what is, for them, probably a rather dull day of grilling nervous candidates.

• Concentrate on listening properly to what the interviewer is saying, rather than fretting about how you are doing and what they might ask next. If you miss something or are confused by a question, it is better to ask for clarification than to waffle on with an inappropriate answer. Keep your answers relevant.

• It is normal to play up your good points and try to skim over the bad ones, but you don't want to look as if you have something to hide. If the interviewer does ask about any area you had hoped to avoid – a previous redundancy, say, or a series of short-term jobs – answer briefly but honestly.

• If you are asked why you want to leave your current job, don't just say you are bored or hate your boss, even if it is true. Couch your reasons in more positive terms: 'I've learned a great deal in the job but now I've reached a stage where there are no immediate promotion prospects and I'm ready to tackle new challenges/take on more responsibility/use talents that are under-used at the moment.'

• Be specific in your answers. If you are asked how you would handle situation X, for example, say how you dealt successfully with a similar situation in the past.

• Employers usually take up references so don't lie about something a referee might be asked to corroborate. In fact, do not lie at all.

• Panel or board interviews can be especially daunting but at least you are less at the whim of one person's likes and dislikes. Sit somewhere where you can see everyone and they can all see you – if the chair is in the wrong place, move it. Members of the panel usually take it in turns to ask questions and you should watch the questioner as they talk to you, then address your answers mainly to him/her, but include the other panel members with occasional eye-contact. At the end, return your gaze to the chairperson. If possible, find out in advance who the members of the panel will be. Try to memorize the names and to be equally polite and friendly to all members, whatever their manner. When it is your turn to ask questions, direct them to the chair, who can redirect them to the appropriate panel member.

• If there is a silence after you have answered a question, don't feel you have to blunder in and fill it. Ask the interviewer if you have made yourself clear and put the ball firmly back in their court.

• If you are asked about your hobbies and interests, don't say anything you can't back up. If you say you are keen on the theatre, for example, expect to be asked about the best play you have seen recently.

• Remember, this is a two-way process: it is a time for you to find out about the potential employer and the job as well as *vice versa*, so don't miss your chance when asked if you have any questions. It also provides another opportunity for you to impress. Prepare three or four intelligent questions that demonstrate your genuine interest in the job or your familiarity with the business and the challenges facing it. Write them down on an index card, if you think you might forget them, and keep it conveniently to hand. If the interviewer doesn't offer you the chance to ask questions, then volunteer, but remember that asking too many is as bad as asking none at all. Be sensitive about time and alert to signs of impatience in the interviewer – remember, the next candidate is probably waiting. If all your questions have been answered during the course of the interview, say so.

• Questions about childcare and marital status are illegal but that doesn't stop some people asking them. If you want the job, it is best to deal with them briefly but assure the interviewer that you can cope and wouldn't have applied for the job otherwise.

• Don't leave the interview without asking how soon you can expect to hear from them.

## Money Matters

Many people accept whatever money is offered in their relief at getting the job, but salary is almost always open to negotiation, providing you go about it in the right way.

Before you go to an interview, try to find out the going rate for such a job. Ask people working in the industry; contact professional associations; look at similar advertisements to see if they mention money.

If you are asked how much you earn now, remember to take into account any perks you may have (subsidized canteen, pension, profit share, interest-free travel loan, medical insurance). Always try to get the employer to mention a figure before you do but if they ask you to say what you are looking for, don't think in terms of what you need but in terms of what the job is worth. Don't give a fixed figure, but a range: 'I'm looking for something in the high twenties' or 'I would hope for a substantial increase on the

£12,000 I'm earning now.' If they give a range, aim for the top.

If the employer is immovable on the money or won't go as high as you would like, think about other areas that might be open to negotiation, such as flexible working hours, an early salary appraisal, training opportunities, a company car.

## After the Interview

Assess your performance and see if you can learn anything from it. What went well? What went badly? If there were any questions that caught you out, brush up your answers for next time. If, despite all your best efforts, the interview was a disaster, don't automatically blame yourself. If you are unlucky enough to land an unpleasant or aggressive interviewer, you will have to write it off to experience and remind yourself that the next one can only be better.

However the interview went, it is a good idea to write the next day, thanking the interviewer for seeing you, reinforcing any important points and adding any extra relevant information you might have forgotten or been unable to pass on at the time. Keep it short and sweet – just enough to nudge the interviewer's memory and show that you really are keen. If you don't hear anything within the time expected, write or call to find out the state of play. Let them know if you have other interviews/offers to consider but don't make it sound like a threat. After the initial enquiry, leave it – hassling only irritates people.

If you are offered the job, clarify all terms and conditions before accepting. If you wait until you are in it before sorting things out, you are in a weaker position to bargain. Don't hand in your notice in your current job until you have something in writing from your new employer: a spoken offer can be withdrawn.

If you don't get the job but are still keen to work for the company, write and say you were sorry to be unsuccessful this time but would like to be kept on file in case of future vacancies. It wouldn't hurt to ask what the person who was appointed had that you didn't, but make it clear that you are just looking for helpful feedback and are not demanding explanations. At least it might give you something useful to take away from the experience rather than viewing it as a total failure.

Keeping up morale is important. It can be discouraging when you apply unsuccessfully for a string of jobs, especially when your friends are all finding their dream jobs, but don't let yourself sink into depression. Treat each interview as practice and remember that if you take great care over your letters and CVs you are already streets ahead of most people. Your time will come.